THE
ILLUSTRATED
HISTORY
OF FOOTBALL

THE ILLUSTRATED HISTORY *OF* FOOTBALL

DAVID SQUIRES

CENTURY

1 3 5 7 9 10 8 6 4 2

Century
20 Vauxhall Bridge Road
London SW1V 2SA

Century is part of the Penguin Random House group of companies
whose addresses can be found at global.penguinrandomhouse.com.

Penguin
Random House
UK

First published by Century in 2016

www.penguin.co.uk

A CIP catalogue record for this book is available from the British Library.

ISBN 9781780895581

Printed and bound in Great Britain by Clays Ltd, St Ives Plc

Penguin Random House is committed to a sustainable future for our business,
our readers and our planet. This book is made from Forest Stewardship Council®
certified paper.

FOR SARAH

CONTENTS

INTRODUCTION

Before the arrival of organised football, people would drift through life, bereft of purpose. Sure, there was cheese-rolling, and the amateur pillaging scene was competitive, but neither quite satisfied the innate human desire to whip a free kick in at the near post.

The little leisure time people had would be spent whittling root vegetables into conversation pieces or tending to the dung bunker. Without recourse to gather in large numbers to grumble about short corners, folk would resort to war and disease as a means of distraction.

Mercifully, the creation of football led to the blissed-out state of utopia the world enjoys today. All aggression famously ended on the day that the rules for football were drafted in a London pub in 1863. Conflicts would now be limited to light-hearted discourse about the length of dagger a gentleman footballer should be permitted to holster upon his knickerbocker hip.

Admittedly, 150 years later, news reports exist purely to catalogue our species' capacity for cruelty and to register the enthusiasm with which we hurtle towards extinction, through a slavish dedication to stupidity, but they have the football results at the end, just before the weather. Hearing those familiar team names and score-lines releases soothing endorphins in the brains of all football fans who don't support Leeds. The modern man would not need to placate himself with eight flagons of mead and a mace fight in the cart park (again, this mostly applies to people who don't support Leeds).

Accounts of football matches from the pre-photography age are captured in timeworn texts, often accompanied by lavish etchings depicting the action. Football and cartoons have also enjoyed a long and happy relationship. Children these days are more interested in their Commodore gamestations and meow meow benders, but this wasn't the case in the early 20th century. Back then, children would tear into a fresh packet of cigarettes, their yellowing eyes glistening in anticipation of finding a card containing a caricature of their favourite player. Didn't find the Fatty Foulkes card? Not to worry, kid, chain-smoke those twenty and have another go!

Later, Roy of the Rovers came along, providing comic escapism to a new generation of football fans. Melchester Rover's Roy Race tapped into the qualities that British football supporters valued most highly in a player. He was heroic, he ran a lot, he usually scored the winning goal and was often suspicious of foreigners. For me, though, despite his occasional lapse into xenophobia, Race was too *clean*. With his helmet of blond He-Man hair and perfect toothy smile, he was the Superman of football and who likes that bloody do-gooder?

There was also the inescapable fact that there was a darker side to football. The first season I became seriously interested in football coincided with what is widely considered to be the grimmest in British football history: 1984/85. Attendances were plummeting, crowd violence was rife and there was a higher than acceptable chance of seeing David Icke on the television. My personal connection between football and cartoons came later, with the discovery of a discarded copy of *Viz* magazine, whilst skiving a school swimming lesson. The pleasure I derived from the hilarious tales of Billy the Fish, the heroic goalkeeper of Fulchester United, was of far greater importance than learning to swim, a skill I would surely never need.

At this time, the fanzine scene in British football was also burgeoning. By the late-eighties, supporters had grown sick of being herded into dangerous, decrepit stadiums and started to organise and protest. Local industrialists who were simply trying to make an honest day's work from milking dry a town's football club were now faced with hundreds of supporters peacefully but vociferously protesting beneath the directors' box. This could be distracting when you're trying to ply a council official with enough Black Forest Gâteau to coerce funds for a roof over the disabled toilets (funds you could then spend on a new conservatory for the summer house).

Humiliatingly, many of the fanzines also contained unflattering cartoons that openly questioned the authority of the people who ran football. My local club was Swindon Town and its fanzine was called *Bring the Noise*, a title that highlighted the obvious links between the sleepy Wiltshire town and the music of Public Enemy. It ran a regular cartoon called 'McBag', which satirised events at Swindon, who at the time were mired in a financial scandal.

It was through the fanzine scene that I was able to get my first cartoon published, in 1992. But this isn't my life story, you can read that in a twenty-volume series that will undoubtedly be published at a later date (or you could just wait for the HBO adaptation). No, this is the story of football, as told over the course of ninetyish cartoons, starting with the earliest kick-abouts of primal man, through to the sophisticated modern era of Jamie Vardy.

You'll read stories of heroes, villains, victories, defeats, stadiums, kits, trophies won and cups stolen, administrators both visionary (Jules Rimet) and foul (almost everyone who followed). Along the way, you'll discover the answers to questions so profound that no-one has even thought to ask them before: what became of Garrincha's dog? Why did Peter Beardsley keep the same hairstyle for over thirty years? What would the world have looked like if Geoff Hurst's goal had been disallowed? How much fun would it be to go on a caravanning holiday with Roy Keane? Plus, there's an exciting window into the future to see what we can expect from the game of tomorrow. You don't get that level of entertainment with your Amstrad entertainment cubes and your Charlie pipes.

I hope you enjoy it, it took me ages.

THE
ILLUSTRATED
HISTORY
OF FOOTBALL

THIGH BONES
FOR GOALPOSTS
EARLY FOOTBALL

From the dawn of human existence, across every continent, human beings have been playing some form of football. In some cases, a bundle of rags would be chased after; in others, an animal bladder rabona-ed. Basic match reports appeared in cave illustrations with primitive paints used to scrawl heat maps and pass-completion stats.

What we do know is that no matter how rudimentary the 'ball', it almost certainly didn't have its own social media account. This may explain why the game took so long to evolve into the much-loved, slickly administered money machine we know today.

This is fun. We should organise a competition against that tribe from the other side of the lava swamp.

Well that's a lovely idea, Justin, but the logistical challenges of organising such an event are simply too great for our primitive brains.

Plus, we're using their leader's head as a ball. So, y' know, awkward.

I suppose.

But one day my vision will be realised and people will travel from far and wide to participate in a challenge to decide the best kicky-skully team in all the land!

THE MAGICAL MAYANS
FOOTBALL IN ANCIENT CULTURES

A form of football was played in many early cultures. Competitive games were played in ancient China and medieval Japan, where a game called *kemari* became popular. *Kemari* was played on a patch of dirt, with trees planted in each corner. To visit a British football stadium in the 1980s was to be unwittingly transported back to twelfth-century Japan. Also, much like British football, the aim of *kemari* was to keep the ball in the air for as long as possible. Historians are divided as to whether visiting fans were also chased back to the bus station by firms of *samurai*, fired-up on primordial glue.

The indigenous people of Australia and North America also played games that involved kicking ball-like objects, and the people of Mesoamerica played using a heavy bouncing ball, crafted from local rubber trees. Contemporary pundits may have remarked upon the latest ball moving too much in the air.

The Spanish conquistadors who arrived in the sixteenth century were spellbound by this exotic ball game and shipped the ball, players and equipment back home to perform in front of King Charles V and other members of the nobility. At first the Castilians were thrilled by their new acquisition and wide-eyed at the prospect of the amount of gold that would swap hands through replica cape sales and duvet covers. But the novelty soon wore off and it wasn't long before the king was publicly courting Aztec imports through the local media.

Wealthy urban aristocrats played a game called *calcio* in Middle Ages Florence. Two teams of twenty-seven players would use their hands and feet to try to shoot the ball into goals at either end, and which ran the width of the sand pitch. If you're thinking that a target that big couldn't be missed even by a medieval Hélder Postiga, you'd be wrong; there were two goalkeepers and an official sitting in a tent to block the path to goal. The removal of tents is another sad indictment on a sport that some believe has lost its soul. AGAINST MODERN CALCIO.

COBBLESTONES AND CORPORAL PUNISHMENT
THE GAME IN BRITAIN

The streets and villages of Britain bore witness to riotous scenes as unruly football matches weaved their destructive path. Numerous monarchs suppressed the game throughout the ages (although Henry VIII did own a pair of football boots). Pottery stalls were overturned, parsnips trampled; the rough game was unpopular with local business owners and heightened the enduring British fear of crimes against property. Just imagine what a rampant pack of muddy serfs crashing through your hamlet would have done for hut prices.

As Britain moved into the nineteenth century, the authorities were also anxious about any congregation of large, violent mobs, given the popular uprisings occurring elsewhere in Europe. What if the players lost their ball in a particularly brambly hedgerow; would their aggression be redirected towards their landowning oppressors?

Eventually the increased urbanisation of an industrialising Britain put pay to this form of the game. Kids turned their backs on the game, preferring to stay indoors, playing with their lethal cotton-spinning machinery and chimneys.

However, football was to be revived through the more refined environs of private schools, famously never an incubator for brutality. It was believed that the playing of games prepared the ruling classes for the wider world, helping them to build character and develop into gentlemen – crucial qualities for any man of breeding to possess when embarking upon an imperial war against poorly armed foreign infidels. Huzzah!

IN BRITAIN, AN ANARCHIC FORM OF THE GAME WAS PLAYED, THE OBJECT OF WHICH WAS TO GET THE BALL FROM ONE END OF A VILLAGE TO THE OTHER IN THE SHORTEST TIME POSSIBLE.

CLEARLY, SUCH AN INELEGANT APPROACH TO FOOTBALL WOULD BE ABHORRENT TO SOPHISTICATED MODERN EYES.

SUCCESSIVE AUTHORITIES, UNIMPRESSED BY SUCH RIOTOUS SCENES, MOVED TO BAN THE SPORT BUT IT RE-EMERGED THROUGH THE PUBLIC SCHOOL SYSTEM IN THE 19TH CENTURY. THIS WAS PART OF A BROADER PHILOSOPHY TO ENCOURAGE BOYS TO PARTICIPATE IN HEALTHY PURSUITS AND DISSUADE THEM FROM SINS OF THE FLESH.

Good heavens, Osborne-Smythe, my manservant could have saved that and he was shot through the brain in the Crimea.

It's not my fault. Sir confiscated my hands to divert me from the wretched path of self-abuse.

Pathetic.

HACKERS
CODIFICATION OF THE GAME

Like all the best ideas, the plan to produce a single code for football was hatched in a pub. In October 1863, a meeting was held at the Freemasons' Tavern in central London. Present that day were representatives from twelve old boys' clubs, who had come together to thrash out an agreement on the laws of the game. Up to that point, each school, university and club was playing to its own set of rules, which made matches against other teams problematic.

The meeting revealed a number of sticking points and the representative from the Blackheath club, Mr Campbell, was particularly concerned about the proposed removal of hacking, remarking: 'You will do away with the courage and pluck of the game, and I will be bound to bring over a lot of Frenchmen who will beat you with a week's practice.'

It became necessary to hold a series of meetings, presumably all in pubs, to iron out these issues. At some point during these gatherings it was decided that the group should be known as the Football Association, as the Wednesday Night Booze and Banter Brigade was already taken.

The secretary, Ebenezer Morley, oversaw the publication of the first rulebook but, at the same time, clubs in Sheffield had developed their own set of rules, to which many schools and universities continued to play. Strange now to think of the Football Association being seen as an irrelevant, London-centric old boys' network, completely out of touch with the needs and opinions of football in the rest of the country, but these were very different times. Eventually though, these differences were resolved and a single set of rules was agreed upon.

CEREMONIAL JAM SPOONS
THE CREATION OF THE FA CUP

Remarkably, there was a time when the FA Cup wasn't an irritating distraction for teams battling to finish eleventh in the Premier League. Indeed, for more than a century, winning it was seen as the pinnacle of achievement for any English football club.

At a meeting of the Football Association in July 1871, secretary CW Alcock proposed that a 'challenge cup' be established, to begin the next season. The FA had fifty member clubs at the time but only fifteen entered, including Queen's Park of Scotland. They got all the way to the semi-final but couldn't afford the travelling expenses to London to play a replay against Wanderers, who received a bye to the final. In fact, owing to other withdrawals, Wanderers had to win only one tie to reach the final.

The first FA Cup final took place on 16 March 1872, at Kennington Oval, between Wanderers and Royal Engineers. The match was watched by 2,000 people and kicked off at 3pm, which became the traditional start and was fine until the mid-2010s when it suddenly became a problem.

Wanderers were captained by CW Alcock himself and won 1–0. Alcock was presented with the inaugural FA Cup at a dinner four weeks later.

The FA Cup quickly grew in popularity and by the mid-1880s it included more than 100 teams, from all over the country. For the first seven years it was contested by old boys, universities and military teams from the south of England. However, the popularity of the game was extending beyond the social elite and Blackburn Rovers' appearance in the 1882 final showed that the sport had spread to the working classes.

As the initiator of this competition— and indeed, the winning captain of the Wanderers— it is my great pleasure to receive the inaugural FA Cup.

THE WANDERERS

Stop that immediately.

Sorry.

GIN

I am personally delighted by the success of the competition, based as it is on the knock-out cup rules of my alma mater.

Now, let us commence with the school tradition whereby the losing team is smeared in hot marmalade and is licked clean by their victors.

Bring out the ceremonial jam spoons!

OK, apparently we aren't doing that now.

In any case, please raise your glasses and drink to the FA Challenge Cup. Long may it be contested exclusively by scholarly gentlemen of breeding.

BUT... NORTHERNERS!!

They call lunch 'dinner'!!

Run for your lives— their snuff boxes aren't even real ivory!

THE FIRST
INTERNATIONAL MATCH
SCOTLAND v ENGLAND, 1872

International competition is great, as it allows us to reinforce cultural differences and legitimises xenophobia. Perhaps you disagree, but then you would, because you're from <insert arbitrary political border within which you happen to have been born>.

That man CW Alcock was instrumental in organising the first international football match, between England and Scotland. Coincidentally, he also arranged the first cricket international between England and Australia, because he was evidently a sporting god, with the facial hair to back it up.

The football match was played on 30 November 1872 at the West of Scotland Cricket Ground, Glasgow. A rope perimeter kept around 4,000 spectators off the pitch and the Scotland fans off the crossbar tape. Scotland wore dark blue shirts with lion crests, white knickerbockers and blue and white hooped socks; England wore white shirts with the three-lion crest, white knickerbockers and blue caps. Both of these kits are more stylish than their current strips, no matter when you are reading this.

There was no Scottish FA at this stage, so Queen's Park agreed to put a side together. The Scotland team consisted entirely of Queen's Park players, which doesn't suggest they undertook an extensive talent search. The England team drew players from nine clubs and CW Alcock had been due to play in the match (OF COURSE HE HAD) but injury forced him to act as one of the 'umpires'. The match ended in a goalless draw, which in no way reflects the footballing abilities of these two proud nations (it does).

THE FORMATION OF THE FOOTBALL LEAGUE
ANOTHER GOOD IDEA CONCEIVED IN A DRINKING ESTABLISHMENT

Before the formation of the Football League, clubs had to rely on cup matches and friendlies for their revenue. The need for consistent income became more pressing after the FA, in 1885, reluctantly permitted professionalism. Restrictions applied though: the first professional to play for England was made to wear blue, while the rest of the team wore white.

A similar scheme might work today for players who laugh exaggeratedly when a throw-in decision goes against them, but with the blue shirt replaced with a suit of rotting donkey organs.

The world's first professional football league was formed in 1888 by Aston Villa director William McGregor. Twelve clubs from the Midlands and North of England were founder members. Preston North End won the first title, along with the FA Cup, without losing a match and became known as The Invincibles. Seven years later, in an act unthinkable from a football chairman, their owner, Billy Sudell, was imprisoned for embezzling funds from the cotton mills he managed to pay his players.

The Football League was expanded to two divisions in 1892 and by 1900 comprised thirty-six teams. Members of the Southern League and northern leagues were incorporated in the early 1920s, creating four professional leagues that would eventually include ninety-two clubs. At no point did any of them demand putting their reserve sides in the lower tiers.

Industrialisation eventually led to increases in workers' wages and leisure time and improvements to transport infrastructure. The new competition proved to be hugely popular and somehow thrived without the need for gimmickry.

1888

This changes everything. No longer shall our clubs struggle for competitive fixtures, we will now have a calendar full of meetings, guaranteeing revenue the year round.

Yes, it is good, but we need to attract people away from their fireplaces and prostitute disassembly kits to attend matches on damp November afternoons in Stoke...

Oh, it's always Stoke with you.

Firstly, I was thinking we could get some dancing girls and—

WHAAA?!

Well, not 'girls' exactly—ladies. And when I say 'dancing', what I really mean is painting gentle watercolours of meadows.

ARTIST'S IMPRESSION

Great Albert's bolt! I can see their ankles!

Oh God, excuse me...

Hm, perhaps it is a little racy. How about some music to entertain the crowd? I took the liberty of booking these shamen to play a tune at the first game.

Love sex intelligence

Comin' on like a seventh sense.

Um, the British Museum are out here. They want their shamen back.

Come on, you two, back to the display case.

Cease this insanity. Let us just adhere to our original plan of an integrated advertising campaign in newspapers and periodicals, with the eventual goal of exploring new growth markets south of West Bromwich.

Fine.

AN ENTIRELY ORIGINAL SPHERE-BASED PASTIME

THE GLOBAL GAME
THE SPREAD OF THE FOOTBALL OVERSEAS

The British Empire stretched to all corners of the globe, generously freeing foreign lands of their natural resources and introducing native people to order, genocide and a ruddy good dose of fair play.

The British also gave the gift of football to the world. The world showed its gratitude by becoming really good at it and ritually humiliating them on the international stage every couple of years or so.

It wasn't just jackbooted imperialists who were spreading the game though. Britain's wealthy industrialists were setting up global operations too, taking with them workers who enjoyed nothing more than a lunchtime kickabout. Teachers, bankers, engineers, dock workers, sailors, miners; all of them plying their profession overseas, all of them displaying the famed British work ethic of whiling away the working hours until they could piss about with their friends.

Local populations adopted the game and, in time, each nation developed its own distinctive football style: the classy passing-sides of central Europe; the trickery of the Brazilians and Argentinians, and the git-based approach of Uruguay.

Football had gone pandemic.

THE UPPER CLASSES OF 19TH CENTURY BRITISH SOCIETY SOUGHT TO INTRODUCE FOOTBALL TO ITS COLONIES, WITH LIMITED SUCCESS...

DINK

DINK

TWAT!

Yes, they're not quite getting this. Perhaps we'll try them with cricket and subjugation.

BUT WEALTHY EX-PAT INDUSTRIALISTS SENT THEIR SONS HOME TO BE EDUCATED AND WHILE IN THE MOTHER COUNTRY THEY DISCOVERED THRILLING NEW GAMES, WHICH THEY WERE KEEN TO RESUME PLAYING UPON THEIR RETURN.

...and then the last one left has to EAT THE BISCUIT!! Ready... set...

Wow! What are these?

What? Oh yeah, you can play with that stuff if you like.

BRITISH-OWNED FACTORIES, MINES, BANKS AND RAILWAY WORKS SPREAD THROUGHOUT LATIN AMERICA AND THEIR WORKERS INTRODUCED FOOTBALL TO THE INTRIGUED LOCAL PEOPLE.

Well, it's better than that biscuit game.

FOOTBALL'S POPULARITY SOON RADIATED ACROSS THE GLOBE AS PEOPLE OF ALL CULTURES WERE SEDUCED BY THE CHARACTERISTICS OF THE GAME THAT CONTINUE TO CHARM US TO THIS DAY:

• BEAUTY

T. IVANOV

• SIMPLICITY

If you refer to section 16 of your yellow folders you'll see that the false libero will play as a deeply inverted nine in the third phase, with a regista becoming a manatee courgette leaf blower.

• COMMERCIAL OPPORTUNITIES

Take two bottles of moustache lubricant into the bathhouse?!

A SHINING BEACON
OF VIRTUE
THE FORMATION OF FIFA

FIFA started out with honourable intentions. Football had been played as a demonstration sport at the 1900 and 1904 Olympics and, with international fixtures becoming increasingly regular, it made sense that a single organisation be formed to oversee the game. The corrupting money that would eventually flow into the sport through its growth and commercialisation would follow but, in 1904, FIFA was just a handful of well-intentioned European men (reflecting a diversity that would echo through the ages).

Comprising several European football associations, FIFA was a collaborative group that had the potential to unite nations to work towards a common goal, and as such it was utterly rejected by British football administrators. They would eventually join and withdraw a couple of times, before settling into the present pattern of going to the meetings, but being completely ignored. It's easy to imagine that when Greg Dyke was the FA's representative, he would take in a box of Krispy Kremes, which would sit uneaten on a trestle table at the back of the room.

The first meeting of FIFA established its founding principles and also decreed that an annual membership fee of fifty French francs was to be paid by each association, thus setting it on a path to sleaze, avarice and stale doughnuts.

We will be a truly global conformation, capable of bringing people together, uniting nations and spreading companionship through our mutual adoration of this glorious game.

Yeah, and then eventually we can become this vast, opaque empire, operating from a ridiculous sci-fi base, from where we can cut all manner of secret deals. Perhaps one day we can organise an international tournament that will evolve into a grotesque, bloated cash cow that craps foul bundles of money into our waxy, grasping hands. Hey, we can impose tax exemptions on host nations and turn a blind eye to so-called 'human rights abuses'. Who knows, perhaps the bidding process will be so underhand that we'll end up having our doors kicked in by a troop of police officers as part of a major international criminal investigation, brought about in part by the evidence of a former executive-turned-informant, whose own wealth is so comedic that he owns a Manhattan penthouse apartment for the exclusive use of his cats. HIS CATS!! Corruption, bribery, money laundering, embezzlement, racketeering, fraud, cynicism, greed: all themes that won't be covered when we tell the story of this fine organisation in a movie that grosses $607 on its opening weekend.

Thanks for your input, the hagiography sounds good, but I'm afraid FIFA will never become the kind of organisation you describe and anyone who suggests otherwise probably deserves to be sued back to the dark ages.

GUÉRIN WAS RIGHT, FIFA TODAY IS MUCH LOVED, ESPECIALLY BY THE YOUNGER GENERATION OF FANS.

What are you doing? Pass the briefcase, fam!

SHIRKERS
AND CANNON FODDER
FOOTBALL AND THE FIRST WORLD WAR

The FA, and football in general, faced widespread criticism when the 1914–15 season went ahead, despite war having been declared. Much of the criticism was based on the concern that men of fighting age would prefer to be playing and watching football, rather than be gassed in a muddy trench. Religious leaders, politicians and the press denounced footballers as self-indulgent shirkers and clubs were accused of helping the enemy by keeping men away from the Western Front.

However, football still had its uses. The FA and clubs made grounds available for military drills and organised recruitment drives at matches. By November 1914, 2,000 of the country's 5,000 professionals had joined up.

As the season progressed, teams and crowds diminished as more men went to war and competitive football was finally suspended in 1915. The final game was the FA Cup final between Sheffield United and Chelsea, which was moved to Old Trafford as the original venue of Crystal Palace was being used by the military.

Hundreds of British footballers were killed or maimed in the war as the horrifying death toll butchered a generation of men and boys. Their sacrifice was not in vain, though, as we now have the freedom to bully TV presenters who don't wear a poppy around the time of Remembrance Day.

UPON THE OUTBREAK OF WAR, THE FOOTBALL AUTHORITIES TOOK ADVICE FROM THE WAR OFFICE AND DECIDED TO COMMENCE WITH THE 1914-15 SEASON.

HOWEVER, PRESSURE SOON BEGAN TO MOUNT FROM THE EDWARDIAN EQUIVALENT OF FACEBOOK.

These MALINGERING, effeminate cowards prance OBSCENELY in their ruby-encrusted chariots while our brave boys play the only game that matters: WAR!

He's right to compare two unrelated things. You wouldn't see rugby players acting like that.

THE LOVE OF FOOTBALL ENDURED, EVEN AT THE FRONT. DURING THE CHRISTMAS DAY TRUCE OF 1914, LEGEND HAS IT THAT AN IMPROMPTU KICK-ABOUT BETWEEN BRITISH AND GERMAN TROOPS TOOK PLACE ON NO MAN'S LAND. BUT SOME HISTORIANS HAVE QUESTIONED THE VERACITY OF CERTAIN DETAILS SURROUNDING THE MATCH.

Run, Kapitän Zeitgeist, the Tommies are closing in like the garbage crusher in Star Wars!

IT HAD BEEN BELIEVED THAT THE WAR WOULD BE OVER BY THIS STAGE, BUT AS IT STRETCHED INTO THE NEW YEAR, IT BECAME CLEAR THAT MORE SOLDIERS WOULD BE NEEDED.

Our strategy of forcing soldiers to charge headlong into a wall of machine gun fire is clearly great, but is taking a toll on our resources.

If only there was a reserve of fit young men experienced at running through quagmires.

Hmmn...

Diversions

FOOTBALL RESULTS

READ THE LATEST EXPLOITS OF A POOL OF ATHLETIC MEN, AGED 16-39

"They will literally do whatever I tell them - Trainer

SHEFFIELD UNITED BEAT CHELSEA 3-0 TO WIN THE 1915 FA CUP FINAL - THE LAST MATCH TO BE PLAYED BEFORE THE SUSPENSION OF FOOTBALL. LORD DERBY - THE MINISTER OF WAR - PRESENTED THE CUP AND GAVE A SPEECH ENCOURAGING ALL PRESENT TO SIGN UP. SO MANY SERVICEMEN WERE IN ATTENDANCE THAT THE EVENT CAME TO BE KNOWN AS THE 'KHAKI FINAL'.

Let's hope that in 100 years' time society will have progressed to the point where military fetishism no longer plays a part in the Cup Final.

THE GREAT INNOVATOR
HERBERT CHAPMAN

Herbert Chapman changed the role of the football manager, controlling tactics, transfers and team selection. He was an innovator, whose legacy stretched beyond on-field success.

He developed tactical responses to rule changes with great success and was an early adopter of the W-M formation. He introduced modern training techniques and championed new ideas such as the use of floodlights, European club competitions, white footballs and numbered shirts. He also had his own column in the *Sunday Express*, which he probably wrote himself. Even as an amateur player, Chapman had been a pioneer, wearing yellow calfskin boots in the belief it would make it easier for team-mates to pick him out.

After success at Northampton Town and Leeds City, he managed Huddersfield Town to two League titles and an FA Cup before, in 1925, he was invited to take over at Arsenal, whom he wanted to turn into 'the Newcastle of the South'. This statement was less amusing in the 1920s.

It took him five years to win Arsenal's first trophy but there was no inter-war equivalent of Piers Morgan to whine on like an entitled crybaby shitehawk.

Chapman's style of play demanded high levels of fitness from his players but drew criticism, as they were masters of soaking up pressure and hurting opponents on the counter-attack. This led to derisive cries of 'lucky Arsenal' from those unaware of the Chapman master plan.

They won the League in 1931, scoring 127 goals in the process – still a club record – and won the title again in 1933.

Chapman set about rebuilding his team and they were four points clear at the top of the table on 30 December 1933. Over the New Year period he caught a cold but felt well enough to go on scouting trips to Bury, Sheffield and Guildford. Tragically, his illness quickly worsened and he died of pneumonia in the early hours of 6 January 1934, aged fifty-five.

THE MANY & VARIOUS INNOVATIONS of HERBERT CHAPMAN

KIT DESIGN

On second thoughts, let's just go with white sleeves.

TEAM TALKS AND TACTICS

KNOCK IT LONG TO THE BIG MAN

Wait, wait. Slow down.

PLAYING RECORDS AT HALF-TIME

Let mee-ee enter-tain you!!

SIGNING FOREIGNERS

Would you...like... a...WOOD...BINE?

I keep telling you, I'm from Bolton.

Anyone?

STADIUM MODIFICATIONS

Here it is, Mr Chapman: a mural to cover an entire end at Highbury. It even plays crowd noises

On second thoughts, let's just go with a clock.

SIGN UP FOR THE ARSENAL BOND SCHEME

GOING OUT WHEN YOU'RE TOO ILL

And now... 'Celebrity X-factor bakers got talent'!

Nope.

THE WHITE HORSE FINAL
BOLTON v WEST HAM, 1923

The Empire Stadium was built as a centrepiece of the 1924 British Empire Exhibition, but also in response to the growing popularity of football and the acknowledgement of the future need to host big events like cup finals, greyhound races and monster truck spectaculars.

The stadium cost £750,000 to construct, the focal point being two ornate towers. Built in the North London area of Wembley, it was conveniently located for everyone who lived in Wembley.

On 28 April 1923, it hosted its first FA Cup final, between Bolton Wanderers of the First Division and West Ham United of the second. Tickets were not required for the match; everyone was welcome to take their chances on the day. An estimated quarter of a million people turned up but the stadium capacity was just 127,000. Two hours before the kick-off, the ground was already full. As more people arrived, spectators flooded on to the pitch. Organisation within the stadium was poor, with most stewards sod-that-for-a-game-of-soldiers-ing.

The roads around the stadium were also packed and the Bolton players and officials had to abandon their team bus a mile from the ground and work their way through the crowds.

A small band of mounted police, aided by the Bolton and West Ham players, worked to edge the crowd back to the perimeter of the pitch. Photographs and newsreels captured the memorable entrance of a white horse called Billy.

THE FOOTBALL AUTHORITIES DRAMATICALLY UNDERESTIMATED THE NUMBER OF PEOPLE WHO WOULD TURN UP TO WATCH THE 1923 FA CUP FINAL AT THE NEWLY-OPENED EMPIRE STADIUM.

ALTHOUGH IT SEEMED THAT MOST OF LONDON HAD CONVERGED ON THE STADIUM, NOT EVERYONE WAS ENTICED TO ATTEND.

Yeah, I was going to go, but the lack of a Gulf State airline plastering its logo all over decades of tradition really put me off. I mean, what's the point without brand penetration for key stakeholders?

Is this the queue for the foam hands?

EVEN THE ALWAYS-EFFICIENT STEWARDS WERE UNABLE TO PREVENT THE UNFOLDING CHAOS AS THOUSANDS OF SPECTATORS SPILLED ON TO THE PITCH.

You're sat in his seat. You can't take photos in here either, it undermines the security of our intellectual property. Also if you didn't buy that sandwich from one of our official outlets you'll have to place it in one of our 'Wember-bins', conveniently located adjacent to the canal of piss that flows along the concourse.

BUT THEN THE ICONIC MOMENT: A GRACEFUL WHITE HORSE CUTTING THROUGH THE CROWD AND PUSHING PEOPLE BACK GENTLY. THANKFULLY, NEWCASTLE HAD BEEN ELIMINATED IN THE FIRST ROUND.

THE ARRIVAL OF KING GEORGE V ALSO SEEMED TO PACIFY THE CROWD, AND IT WAS HE WHO PRESENTED THE CUP TO WINNERS BOLTON. GEORGE WASN'T A SPORTS FAN, BUT HAD BEEN THE FIRST RULING MONARCH TO ATTEND A FOOTBALL MATCH, THIS IN AN AGE BEFORE PUBLIC FIGURES WERE DUTY BOUND TO BE FOOTIE NUTS.

Come on, the Bolton Hammers!

#1 FAN

THE FIRST WORLD CUP
URUGUAY 1930

Curious to think that there was a time before people could punctuate their lives with international football tournaments. Recalling bygone World Cups helps us to remember our personal history and our state of being at those four-yearly junctions. For example, mine goes:

1986: taste Cherry Coke for the first time.
1990: score work experience at Radio Rentals in the mistaken belief it would enable me to watch the entire World Cup on a big wall of televisions.
1994: student.
1998: unemployed.
2002: drunk.
2006: fat.
2010: try Cherry Coke again. Not as nice as I remembered.
2014: write to Radio Rentals to ask if they need any work experience staff.

Before World Cups, life was harder and people had to use grimmer touchstones to recall life events (1918: the insane theatre of war. 1922: lancing buboes. 1926: dead).

Thankfully, as ever, FIFA was at hand to provide levity. Uruguay won the right to host the first World Cup with a generous bid. It planned to build a new stadium – Estadio Centenario – to host every game. When finished it would be an impressive structure, featuring a 150-metre tower, rising above the north side. However, a harsh winter in Montevideo delayed progress, meaning that the tournament's early matches would need to be played at smaller, local, venues. When the new stadium opened for Uruguay's first match, an impressed Jules Rimet declared it to be the finest football stadium in the world.

It didn't matter that spectators were forced to negotiate a construction site littered with building materials, because it was before the bloody PC, health and safety brigade banned people from being crushed to death in workplace accidents. Back then, people were crushed all the time and it never did them any harm. Bloody clipboard-brandishing bloody fun police. Clarkson's right, you can't even have Easter eggs any more. Thanks a lot, the EU.

FIGHTING AS AN OFFICER IN THE FIRST WORLD WAR WAS JULES RIMET, WHO WOULD GO ON TO BE ELECTED FIFA PRESIDENT IN 1921.

There has to be a better way of settling international conflicts.

I envision a day where warring nations will settle their differences in the sporting arena, in an atmosphere of mutual respect and friendship.

You should probably be wearing a gas mask, sir.

And there will be music and dance and individually-branded team buses...

HIS DREAM WAS REALISED IN 1928 WHEN FIFA AGREED TO HOLD A WORLD CHAMPIONSHIP. THEY CONVENED AGAIN A YEAR LATER TO DECIDE UPON A FITTING HOST. BIDS WERE RECEIVED FROM SEVERAL COUNTRIES, BUT IT WAS URUGUAY'S TENDER THAT WAS SUCCESSFUL.

We'll provide free tram transport to matches for fans who present valid match tickets.

NEDERLAND

We have the world's finest cathedrals and churches. Competing teams will go on a spiritual journey.

ITALIA

We'll present each team with a platter of delicious cured meats.

ESPAÑA

Sweden will give all players free, unlimited access to the Gothenburg Elk Museum.

SVERIGE

Despite the crippling global economic depression, we'll pay the travel and accommodation costs of all players and officials and build a vast new stadium at huge public expense.

URUGUAY

ESPAÑA   NEDERLAND   ITALIA
URUGUAY

THE FIRST WORLD CUP GOAL
LUCIEN LAURENT CRACKS ONE IN

With just a month to go before the start of the World Cup, the tournament was short of one crucial element: participants. There wasn't a single European entrant and it took some severe pressure from the governing body to convince France, Belgium and Yugoslavia to travel. Romania's involvement was the result of an intervention from their newly crowned monarch, King Carol II, a keen football fan. Egypt had also been due to participate but missed their connecting ship and had to withdraw.

France's Lucien Laurent had enjoyed the fifteen-day journey across the Atlantic aboard a cruise ship. The Peugeot Sochaux forward passed the time in the swimming pool or cinema and the mornings were spent being entertained by a violinist and a comedian. Perhaps two weeks of listening to the same jokes instilled in him a fire that made him impervious to the freezing conditions in Montevideo, enabling him to become the first person to score a World Cup goal.

There was a wild disparity between FIFA's retrospective estimation of some of the tournament's attendance figures and those given by Uruguayan officials. For this opening fixture, against Mexico, the attendance was announced to be 4,444, which suggests they weren't trying very hard that day.

FRANCE SAILED TO MONTEVIDEO ABOARD THE SS CONTE VERDE- AN ITALIAN CRUISE LINER. THEY WERE JOINED ON THE 15-DAY JOURNEY BY TEAMS FROM BELGIUM AND ROMANIA, AS WELL AS A VARIETY OF REFEREES AND FIFA OFFICIALS, INCLUDING JULES RIMET, WHO TRAVELLED WITH THE WORLD CUP TROPHY CLOSELY-GUARDED.

Hey, Rimet's distracted, let's look at the trophy.

Huh? Where is it?

You don't want to know.

ON 13 JULY 1930, THE FIRST MATCHES OF THE INAUGURAL WORLD CUP WERE PLAYED. FRANCE TOOK ON MEXICO AT THE ESTADIO POCITOS, WITH BELGIUM AND THE USA KICKING OFF TEN MINUTES LATER ACROSS TOWN. WHEN THE FIXTURES WERE BEING DRAWN UP, THE FRENCH TEAM REQUESTED THAT THEIR GAME BE PLAYED FIRST, IN ORDER FOR THEM TO CELEBRATE BASTILLE DAY THE NEXT DAY.

It makes sense for us to binge eat mid-tournament. Cake and wine thicken an athlete's blood, making him stronger, faster.

And these cigarettes massage the lungs. I can actually feel them massaging my lungs.

INSPIRED BY THE PROSPECT OF A PARTY, FRANCE COMFORTABLY WON 4-1. THEIR INSIDE-RIGHT, LUCIEN LAURENT, SCORED THE FIRST EVER WORLD CUP GOAL WITH A NINETEENTH-MINUTE VOLLEY.

LAURENT WAS, IN 1998, THE ONLY SURVIVING MEMBER OF THE 1930 SQUAD TO SEE THE WORLD CUP LIFTED BY FRANCE'S WONDERFUL TEAM OF MULTI-ETHNIC PLAYERS: THE KIND OF THING THAT OLD PEOPLE ARE ALWAYS COOL WITH.

Call the police.

VICTORY OR DEATH
URUGUAY WIN THE WORLD CUP

A capacity crowd crammed into Montevideo's new stadium to witness the first World Cup final, between Uruguay and Argentina. Those who couldn't gain access listened anxiously outside, trying to deduce the score from the roar of the fans, which never works.

The teams were accompanied to the stadium by a cavalcade of police officers and soldiers, amid rumours that snipers had been hired to shoot players from both sides. Uruguay settled more quickly and turned early pressure into a goal in the twelfth minute, Pablo Dorado shooting past Juan Botasso, who was to put in a textbook display of ineffective 1930s Pathé newsreel goalkeeping.

But Argentina rallied and eight minutes later Carlos Peucelle equalised. Worse was to follow for the hosts on thirty-seven minutes; Guillermo Stábile racing on to a long, defence-splitting Luis Monti pass and knocking the ball home to give Argentina a half-time lead.

During the interval, Uruguayan officials congratulated their team for successfully subduing the passionate crowd. Captain José Nasazzi ground his teeth to chalky stumps and Uruguay re-emerged with renewed vim.

Pedro Cea levelled the scores after fifty-seven minutes and Santos Iriarte gave them the lead with a long-range effort eleven minutes later. The home crowd was convinced the cup was theirs and many crawled under the perimeter fence and on to the pitch. Héctor Castro added a fourth in the final minute before the Belgian referee, John Langenus, blew the final whistle and legged it to a waiting car, which raced him to the port. The fans outside kicked themselves that they had missed a 16–11 goalfest.

The following day was declared a national holiday in Uruguay but the mood was less jovial in Buenos Aires, where an angry mob threw stones at the Uruguay consulate. The two football associations consequently broke off all relations and the two teams didn't play each other for another two years.

URUGUAY'S RIGOROUS PREPARATIONS BEGAN EIGHT WEEKS BEFORE THE TOURNAMENT STARTED. THEIR COACH, ALBERTO SUPPICI, GATHERED THE SQUAD AT A FOREST RETREAT, WHERE HE IMPOSED A STRICT REGIME OF RULES AND CURFEWS.

Ooh, I've read about these places. They give you a 'dignity detox'. It's supposedly uh-mazing!

TEN BOATS WERE CHARTERED TO TAKE ARGENTINA FANS ACROSS THE RIVER PLATE TO THE FINAL, BUT THOUSANDS MORE WENT TO THE PORT TO TRY AND GET ABOARD, SETTING OFF FIRE-WORKS AND CHANTING 'VICTORIA O MUERTE!' (VICTORY OR DEATH!)

Heh. Death? Really? Bit extreme don't you think? After all, it's only a game. Death? Come on...

Death! Definitely death!

Ok then...

SUPPORTERS WERE SEARCHED FOR GUNS UPON ARRIVAL AT THE ESTADIO CENTENARIO, BUT WITH THE POLICE DISTRACTED, MANY PEOPLE WERE ABLE TO SLIP BY AND GAIN ENTRY.

What the hell is this?

A yoga mat. Well, I use it more for Pilates really.

Why do you have this?

Well, if you can think of a better way to align the pelvis, I'd like to hear it.

IN THE ARGENTINA DRESSING ROOM NEWS EMERGED THAT DEATH THREATS HAD BEEN SENT TO KEY PLAYER LUIS MONTI AND HIS MOTHER. 'I'LL BE DAMNED IF I'M GOING TO BE A MARTYR FOR A GAME OF FOOTBALL', HE SUPPOSEDLY SAID, BUT LATER RELENT-ED AND AGREED TO PLAY.

Stupid boy!

SLAP!

Aw Mum..!

BEFORE THE GAME COULD START IT BECAME NECESSARY TO SETTLE AN ARGUMENT OVER WHICH TEAM'S FOOTBALL WOULD BE USED. A COMPROMISE WAS MET WHEREBY THE BALL WOULD BE SWAPPED AT HALF-TIME.

Our ball is crafted from the finest Uruguayan leather, clearly it is better

FIFA

Nonsense! The latest manufacturing technology was used to make our ball.

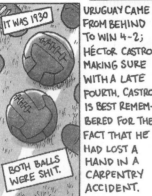

IT WAS 1930

BOTH BALLS WERE SHIT.

URUGUAY CAME FROM BEHIND TO WIN 4-2; HÉCTOR CASTRO MAKING SURE WITH A LATE FOURTH. CASTRO IS BEST REMEM-BERED FOR THE FACT THAT HE HAD LOST A HAND IN A CARPENTRY ACCIDENT.

You are brave, my friend. We will call you 'El manco', or 'the one-armed'.

Yeah, or you could just call me Héctor.

YOU WOULDN'T HEAR A URUGUAYAN PLAYER USING INSULTING NICK-NAMES THESE DAYS. ANYWAY, UPON THE FINAL WHISTLE, THE REFEREE RACED OFF TO A WAITING CAR AND THE JUBILANT CROWD SWARMED ON TO THE PITCH.

Mum...?

DAS WUNDERTEAM
AUSTRIA IN THE 1930s

The coffee houses of Vienna were places for the middle classes to meet, gossip and debate politics, art, culture and string quartets they were into way before you. While wondering silently whether their contemporaries had noticed their new cravats, urbane Austrians would also discuss the new obsession of central Europe: football.

While some cafés may have been themed around breakfast cereals or children's toys, it was football that dominated the conversations of patrons at the Ring Café. Their enthusiasm was heightened by the exploits of the brilliant Austrian national team, built by their visionary coach Hugo Meisl.

The first hero of the coffee house was striker Josef Uridil, a bustling striker nicknamed 'The Tank'. He was so popular that he became the subject of a cabaret song and his image was used in numerous advertising campaigns. His proletarian roots made him popular with the café dwellers, who perhaps exaggerated how much they liked him in order to overemphasise their own working-class roots.

However, after narrowly missing out on winning the excellently named Dr Gerö Cup – a lengthy competition involving Czechoslovakia, Italy, Hungary and Switzerland – the patrons of the Ring Café clamoured for the selection of their new hero, Matthias Sindelar. He was a wispy, intelligent centre-forward, so fragile that he became nicknamed 'The Paperman'; living proof that you don't have to be big and tough to be good at sport. Meisl was now faced with a selection headache, which may have just been caffeine withdrawal. Either way, the solution lay in the coffee house.

IN 1931, AUSTRIA'S COACH HUGO MEISL WAS FACED WITH A TEAM SELECTION DILEMMA. HIS FRIEND AND MENTOR JIMMY HOGAN ACCOMPANIED HIM TO THE FAMOUS RING CAFE TO TAP INTO THE COLLECTIVE KNOWLEDGE OF THE VIENNESE FOOTBALL INTELLIGENTSIA...

NO WIRELESS, GUYS. MAKE LIKE IT'S 1889 AND TALK TO EACH OTHER! #SORRYNOTSORRY #YUMMYCOFFEE

You sure about this, Jimmy?

I'm telling you, these people are smart.

Two egg specials, please.

Sick, sick...

What?

Shh, listen, Hugo...

Did you hear the Austria Wien match last night?

God no, I tuned in to a livestream of a Prussian youth cup game.

Oh yeah, I used to do that, but I've moved on to a more technical form of the game whereby a smaller, harder ball is used. Use of the feet is prohibited, which encourages movement. It's called 'cricket'. You probably haven't heard of it.

Guys, it says here that a band I liked before you is playing in a cool bunker in Innsbruck next Tuesday.

Let me see the paper, man.

'The Paper Man'. I understood that! They want me to recall Sindelar. Of course!

You see, Hugo, it's like I told you: anyone who rides a penny-farthing with ribbons on the handlebars must know what they're talking about.

MEISL WAS RIGHT TO LISTEN. OVER THE NEXT TWO YEARS, MATTHIAS SINDELAR SCORED 16 GOALS IN 16 MATCHES AS AUSTRIA THRASHED SUCCESSIVE OPPONENTS, EARNING THEMSELVES THE NICKNAME 'DAS WUNDERTEAM'.

Two egg specials, yeah.

Jesus.

MUSSOLINI'S WORLD CUP
ITALY, 1934

As hard as it is to believe that FIFA would award World Cup hosting rights to a brutal dictatorship, that's exactly what they did in 1934. Less surprising is the fact that the whole event descended into a big old Fascist rally, with large crowds of people chanting *'Duce! Duce!'*, demonstrating a love for their leader that would surely never fade. Before each of Italy's matches, players and match officials would all give the right-arm salute. On the surface, this would appear to confirm all assumptions about the kind of people who become referees, but it's doubtful they were given much of a choice.

The national team carried the hallmarks of the regime and their march to victory was characterised by bullying and intimidation and was cloaked in the stench of suspicion. Opposition goals were disallowed bizarrely (such as Spain's Lafuente dribbling past four Italians to score, only to have the goal ruled out for offside), foul play was overlooked and referees were routinely summoned to meet Mussolini before matches.

Still, you can only beat the unfairly disadvantaged team that's put in front of you and the authoritarian coach Vittorio Pozzo had a well-drilled squad with some genuinely world-class players.

In the final, Czechoslovakia looked set to ruin the dictator's big day. Antonín Puč gave them an early lead, but a late Raimundo Orsi equaliser sent the match into extra-time. Angelo Schiavio's goal settled it for Italy, annoyingly.

At the final whistle Pozzo was chair-lifted off the pitch and the Italian captain, Giampiero Combi, was presented with the World Cup, along with the Copa del Duce – a massive, ostentatious trophy commissioned by the dictator himself. Each player also received a signed photograph of Mussolini. Bloody hell, Czechoslovakia, couldn't you have held out for eight more minutes?

THE BATTLE OF HIGHBURY
ENGLAND v ITALY, 1934

'I'll fockin' see you out there', snarls Ted Drake in his familiar Cork accent, jabbing an angry finger towards a smirking Giuseppe Meazza. The mood in the players' tunnel at Highbury is tense; referee Graham Poll steps in to calm an incident I may have confused with a later one. Gunnersaurus Rex assesses the situation impassively.

The arrival of Pozzo's world champions on a foggy London afternoon had caused a stir. The English press revealed that Mussolini had offered handsome cash rewards and an Alfa Romeo for each Italian player if they were to return victorious. The dictator received regular updates on the score and you can only feel sympathy for the minion tasked with informing him that England were 3–0 up within fifteen minutes.

There were seven Arsenal players in the England team, as well as a young Stanley Matthews, who was making only his second international appearance. The match took its toll on both teams, who spent the afternoon hacking at each other enthusiastically. Luis Monti was crocked for Italy, while England's Eddie Hapgood had his nose broken. Ray Bowden damaged his ankle, Ted Drake was punched and Eric Brook ended the day with a fractured arm.

The visitors clawed back two second-half goals, but it wasn't enough to spare another quivering minion shuffling off to Il Duce's office, telegram in hand.

IN NOVEMBER 1934, VITTORIO POZZO BROUGHT HIS ITALY SIDE TO LONDON TO PLAY ENGLAND IN WHAT WAS BILLED AS THE UNOFFICIAL WORLD TITLE DECIDER. AS A YOUNGER MAN, THE ANGLOPHILE POZZO STUDIED IN ENGLAND, WHERE HE ALSO OBSERVED MODERN FOOTBALL TRAINING TECHNIQUES.

THE MATCH ALSO PROVIDED THE OPPORTUNITY TO SCORE POINTS IN THE PROPAGANDA BATTLEGROUND OF 1930s EUROPE.

Sweet Remus! Have you seen what the English papers are saying?

ITALY MAY HAVE WON THE WORLD CUP ON MERIT BUT THEY ARE NO MATCH FOR OUR UNERRING SENSE OF SUPERIORITY

Hmm. This one is quite complimentary.

Daily Mail
Hurrah for the Blackshirts

Oh. Yeah. That's not mine. Bit too right wing for my liking. My parents left it here. They say they get it for the word puzzles. I mean, I've told them, but what can you do...?

ENGLAND GOT OFF TO A FLYING START AND WERE AWARDED A PENALTY IN THE FIRST MINUTE. HOWEVER, ERIC BROOK'S SPOT-KICK WAS SAVED ACROBATICALLY BY CARLO CERESOLI.

Ye Gods, are there no depths to which these crafty Italians will not stoop?

ITALY FACED A SERIOUS SETBACK WHEN INFLUENTIAL MIDFIELDER LUIS MONTI BROKE HIS FOOT, EFFECTIVELY REDUCING THEM TO TEN MEN. ENGLAND RACED INTO A 3-0 LEAD AND IT TOOK UNTIL HALF-TIME FOR POZZO TO MAKE A TACTICAL INTERVENTION.

Eat this and skull this...

MEAZZA SCORED TWO SECOND-HALF GOALS BUT ENGLAND HELD ON. YET IT IS THE BRUTALITY OF THE MATCH THAT IS BEST REMEM-BERED, WITH UNDIGNIFIED SCENES NEVER AGAIN SEEN WITHIN THE REFINED SUR-ROUNDINGS OF HIGHBURY.

Boss! Tony's ram-raided the ticket office, Ray's filled the North Bank with prawn crackers and Merse has left something awful on the Herbert Chapman bust.

Quiet for a Tuesday.

IN THE AFTERMATH, SOME SECTIONS OF THE PRESS DEMANDED THAT ENGLAND WITHDRAW FROM INTERNATIONAL MATCHES. AN OVERREACTION PERHAPS, BUT IT WOULD HAVE SPARED A LOT OF EXISTENTIAL ANGST FURTHER DOWN THE LINE.

TOTALITARIAN FOOTBALL
THE 1938 WORLD CUP

Pozzo's new-look team played their first-round tie against Norway in Marseilles. With 10,000 Italian political exiles in attendance, the players' Fascist salute during the national anthems went down about as well as could be expected. Intimidated, the players began to lower their arms, but Pozzo convinced them to resume their salute, believing a powerful psychological point could be scored.

Incidents like these led many to believe that Pozzo was a Fascist himself, but documents emerged in the 1990s to reveal that he had helped the anti-Fascist resistance during the war and aided the escape of Allied prisoners of war.

If there had been suspicion about Italy's 1934 championship, the manner in which they claimed victory in 1938 proved beyond doubt that they were the best team in the world.

Pozzo remains the only man to have retained the World Cup, and stayed on as Italy's coach until 1948. During nineteen years of service, he didn't receive a penny of payment. Instead, he made a living from journalism and lived a simple life. For example, he never owned a television set. Have you seen Italian television, though? Not a massive sacrifice, that one.

Quick to capitalise upon the success, Mussolini gathered the team in Rome two weeks later for a photo shoot, kitting the squad out in sailor outfits. As despicable as he undoubtedly was, one has to admire his sense of style.

ONLY GIUSEPPE MEAZZA AND GIOVANNI FERRARI WERE LEFT FROM THE ITALIAN TEAM THAT HAD WON THE CUP IN 1934, WITH POZZO FAVOURING PLAYERS FROM ITALY'S 1936 OLYMPICS-WINNING SQUAD. MUSSOLINI SAW THEM OFF TO FRANCE WITH A TYPICALLY INSPIRING MESSAGE:

Win or die. LOLOLOLOLOLOL!!!

AN ATMOSPHERE OF BROODING CONFLICT HUNG HEAVILY OVER THE TOURNAMENT AS EUROPE EDGED CLOSER TO WAR. IN PARIS, ANTI-FASCIST DEMONSTRATORS AND POLITICAL EXILES SHOWERED THE GERMAN PLAYERS WITH BOTTLES AND OLD FRUIT WHEN THEY GAVE THE NAZI SALUTE BEFORE THEIR GAME WITH SWITZERLAND.

Hey, are you lot not going to salute too? If you stick your arms up, we'll give you half our match fee...

No thank you. We Swiss will never profit from the spoils of Nazism.

TENSIONS ALSO RAN HIGH BEFORE ITALY'S QUARTER-FINAL WITH FRANCE; A DISPUTE BREAKING OUT OVER WHICH TEAM WOULD CHANGE FROM THEIR TRADITIONAL BLUE SHIRTS:

We are reigning world and Olympic champions. Everyone recognises the famous Azzurri. It would be sacrosanct for us to change!

So what? We are the hosts! Surely you cannot imagine Les Bleus would wear any other colour in our own capital city?

Guys, guys, guys. Relax! I have the perfect solution...

Blackshirts!

THAT WAS HIS ANSWER FOR EVERYTHING.

ITALY WERE CLEARLY THE BEST TEAM IN THE WORLD AND WERE WORTHY CHAMPIONS, OVER-COMING HUNGARY 4-2 IN THE FINAL TO CLAIM THE TITLE. MEAZZA COLLECTED THE TROPHY FROM THE FRENCH PRESIDENT AND A DELIGHTED IL DUCE SET TO WORK ON HIS NEXT PROJECT.

If we're this good at calcio, we'll be even better at war! If I'm wrong then let me meet a violent and bloody death at the hands of my own people!

JOE GAETJENS' FINEST HOUR
USA 1 ENGLAND 0, 1950

England's defeat to Iceland at Euro 2016 was embarrassing, but nowhere near as shocking as the events that took place at the Estádio Independência, Belo Horizonte, Brazil in 1950, when the United States' team of pot-washers and postmen created perhaps the biggest shock in World Cup history.

England boasted an impressive post-war record and came into the finals looking to confirm their status as the world's best. USA's form was less impressive. They qualified by beating Cuba – their first win in a recognised international in fifteen years. Some other stuff had been going on during that time, though.

Not all of the US team were strictly 'American'. The scorer of the winning goal – Joe Gaetjens – wasn't a US citizen (he was from Haiti), neither was their captain, Eddie McIlvenny (a Scot). Joe Maca had even played for Belgium against England in 1946, prompting England winger Jimmy Mullen to ask of him, 'how many countries do you play for?'

News of the shock failed to make much of a splash in England, with the sports pages instead focusing on the England cricket team's first home series defeat by the West Indies. The result received little attention in the States either. Only one self-funded journalist, from the *St Louis Post-Dispatch*, had made the journey, but he was called Dent McSkimming, which makes up for it. People don't call their kids Dent any more.

The 2005 film *The Game of Their Lives* told the story of the match and stars Gerard Butler, always a mark of quality. The film's portrayal of the England team gave the impression that it had been picked from members of the Bullingdon Club. Weirdly, Gavin Rossdale, the lead singer of Bush, played Stan Mortensen. The part of Dent McSkimming was played by Patrick Stewart, who must have been between Star Trek conventions.

CHAMPIONS-ELECT ENGLAND GRACED THE WORLD CUP WITH THEIR PRESENCE FOR THE FIRST TIME IN 1950. THE FA TOOK THE COMPETITION SO SERIOUSLY THAT IT SENT A SOLITARY DELEGATE AND PACKED STANLEY MATTHEWS OFF TO CANADA TO PLAY IN AN EXHIBITION MATCH, FORCING HIM TO MISS THE START OF THE TOURNAMENT.

Look, Stan, we need to save you for the open-top bus celebrations...

hm

THE UNITED STATES TEAM, MEANWHILE, WAS MADE UP OF SEMI-PROFESSIONALS. AMONG THEIR RANKS WERE A POSTMAN, A HEARSE DRIVER AND A DISH-WASHER. MOST OF THEM PLAYED IN THE ST. LOUIS LEAGUE, WHICH AT THE TIME ONLY PLAYED 30-MINUTE HALVES.

Two minutes, guys. There are some Twinkies in the glove box, help yourselves, yeah.

STILL, THE U.S. PLAYERS WERE UNDAUNTED BY THE PEDIGREE OF THEIR ENGLISH OPPONENTS AND ARRIVED AT THE STADIUM IN BELO HORIZONTE WEARING STETSON HATS AND CHEWING ON CIGARS.

I am so goddamn sick of the stereotypical representation of Americans in the media.

Yee-ha. I'm not even American and look at the state of me.

ENGLAND PEPPERED THE US GOAL WITH SHOTS, BUT IT WAS THE UNDERDOGS WHO TOOK THE LEAD WHEN A MISHIT SHOT WAS DIVERTED INTO THE NET VIA THE HEAD OF JOE GAETJENS.

THERE WERE 10,000 SPECTATORS IN THE GROUND AT THE START OF THE GAME, BUT BY THE TIME THE FINAL WHISTLE BLEW, THE CROWD HAD SWOLLEN TO 40,000 AS WORD SPREAD THROUGHOUT THE CITY OF THE ENORMOUS SHOCK UNFOLDING...

This I have to see! A once-in-a-lifetime chance to see England humiliated at sport!

Run! It's the equivalent of England beating the USA at baseball, gun crime or compelling TV drama!

THE ECSTATIC FANS SET OFF FIREWORKS AND LIT BONFIRES, OTHERS CARRIED THE VICTORIOUS AMERICAN PLAYERS OFF THE PITCH UPON THEIR SHOULDERS.

Everything has changed!

IN ENGLAND THE UPSET RECEIVED LITTLE COVERAGE AND WAS SEEN AS A FREAK RESULT RATHER THAN AN INDICATION OF A FORMER FOOTBALL POWER IN DECLINE.

Nothing has changed!

SHOCKING FOOTBALL NEWS!

Stanley Matthews enthrals Canada as the empire flexes its muscles again.

THE MARACANAZO
BRAZIL 1 URUGUAY 2, 1950

After conceding the goal that cost Brazil the 1950 World Cup, goalkeeper Moacir Barbosa became a focus for public recrimination. He was still suffering abuse years after he'd been beaten at his near post. In 1963, he was gifted with the goalposts from that fateful match. It's hard to know what to buy for national pariahs, isn't it? Vouchers is one option, physical reminders of life-defining trauma is another. Not unreasonably, he took them home and tossed them on his barbecue. 'The steak I cooked that day was the best steak I ever tasted,' he said, unperturbed by the paint fumes.

Brazil had gone into the decisive match of the 1950 World Cup as clear favourites. That morning, the Brazilian newspaper *O Mundo* printed a photo of the Brazil team, with the caption, 'These are the world champions'. Uruguay's captain, Obdulio Varela, bought as many copies as he could, spread them on his hotel bathroom floor and encouraged his team-mates to shower them in hot piss.

Even the president of the Uruguayan FA had low expectations, telling the squad that limiting Brazil to four goals would be a successful outcome. But Uruguay's players had more self-belief. Inside-right Julio Pérez was so worked up that he wet himself during the national anthem. There's a lot of urine in this story.

Brazil's pre-match hubris appeared to have been justified when Friaça put the hosts ahead just after half-time. The 200,000 people who had wedged into the newly-built Maracanã knew their team were world champions. Nothing could stop them now, this was their dest... oh wait, Schiaffino has equalised.

Brazil were suddenly overcome with nervous exhaustion and folded under the weight of expectation. With eleven minutes left, Ghiggia darts into the area and slams home the goal to win the cup for Uruguay. A wisp of white dust flies up as the ball crosses the line. Silence echoes throughout the stadium. Newspapers drift across the emptying terraces, and a housekeeper sighs at the mess the Uruguay team have left on one of the bathroom floors. At least it's only wee, she thinks. But she hasn't checked behind the door.

BEFORE THE DECIDING MATCH OF THE 1950 WORLD CUP, THE STATE GOVERNOR OF RIO, ÀNGELO MENDES DE MORAES, ADDRESSED THE PACKED CROWD AT THE NEWLY-BUILT MARACANÃ. BRAZIL NEEDED JUST A DRAW TO CLAIM THE TITLE, BUT IN THE 79TH MINUTE, WITH THE GAME POISED AT 1-1, URUGUAY'S ALCIDES GHIGGIA BURST INTO THE BRAZILIAN PENALTY AREA AND THE WORDS OF THE GOVERNOR LINGERED HEAVILY, LIKE A FART IN A COMMUTER CARRIAGE:

'You Brazilians,

who I consider victors of the tournament...

You players,

who in less than a few hours

Gol do Uruguay.
Gol do Uruguay?
Gol do Uruguay.

Will be acclaimed champions by millions of your compatriots

You who have no equals in the terrestrial hemisphere

You who are superior to every other competitor

you who I already salute as conquerors.'

Oh well, at least nothing this humiliating will happen to Brazil at a World Cup on home soil again.

Amen to that.

THE MATTHEWS FINAL
BLACKPOOL 4 BOLTON 3, 1953

Stanley Matthews was already approaching middle age by the time he inspired the most memorable comeback in FA Cup history. This would appear to give hope to us all, but by 1953 Matthews already had an impressive playing career behind him and he wasn't just spotted playing five-a-side on a Thursday night in Blackpool.

When his father was on his deathbed in 1945, he made Stanley promise two things. Firstly, to look after his mother (reasonable), and secondly to win the FA Cup (ah). The dutiful son tried his best, helping The Tangerines to two cup finals in 1948 and 1951, but they fell short on both occasions. The 1953 final didn't start well for them either. Bolton took the lead after just 75 seconds via Footballer of the Year, Nat Lofthouse, who had scored in every round.

Stan Mortenson equalised after 35 minutes, but Bolton regained the lead just four minutes later through Willie Moir. Ten minutes into the second half, Eric Bell made it 3–1, despite playing with a torn hamstring. All seemed lost.

Enter Stanley. After Matthews had turned the game on its head, the Bolton players could only stand and applaud. The Blackpool team paraded him around the pitch on their shoulders and he allowed himself a rare taste of alcohol from the champagne-filled FA Cup. However, this didn't result in a Barney Gumble-style booze freak-out and he went on to play professional football until he was fifty.

Matthews returned to Wembley a few months later to represent England against Hungary, along with three other members of the Blackpool team. Another glorious day saw England emerge with three lovely goals.

THE BRITAIN OF 1953 WAS ALMOST UNRECOGNISABLE FROM TODAY. IT WAS A TIME OF AUSTERITY, CHILD POVERTY AND SUSPICION OF FOREIGNERS.

Eat your spam fritters or all those economic migrants will come and radicalise you.

Eh?

TELEVISION SETS WERE BECOMING AN INCREASINGLY COMMON SIGHT IN BRITISH LIVING ROOMS, THOUGH, AND THE 1953 CUP FINAL WAS THE FIRST TO DRAW A MASS VIEWING AUDIENCE. FEW YET REALISED HOW THIS INVENTION WOULD REVOLUTIONISE OUR LIVES.

EGGHEADS

THE FINAL WAS BLACKPOOL'S THIRD IN SIX YEARS. THEY'D LOST THE PREVIOUS TWO AND LOOKED SET FOR MORE HEARTACHE AS THEY TRAILED BOLTON 3-1 AFTER 55 MINUTES.

I couldn't be more hurt if the chairman sent me an offensive telegram.

BFC

BUT THEN STANLEY MATTHEWS TOOK CONTROL, CREATING HAVOC ON THE RIGHT WING, EXPOSING THE INJURED ERIC BELL AND THE TIRING RALPH BANKS.

Spam fritters were a mistake.

HIS INTERVENTION ENABLED BLACKPOOL TO PULL LEVEL – PLAYING A KEY ROLE IN TWO OF STAN MORTENSEN'S THREE GOALS – AND HE THEN CROSSED FOR BILL PERRY TO HEAD IN AN INJURY-TIME WINNER. MUCH TO HIS EMBARRASSMENT, THE MATCH BECAME KNOWN AS 'THE MATTHEWS FINAL', OVERSHADOWING THE EFFORTS OF MORTENSEN, WHO REMAINS THE ONLY PLAYER TO SCORE A HAT-TRICK IN A WEMBLEY FA CUP FINAL.

Come on, Stan, climb up here.

Oh, well, I really don't..

Right. Yeah. Course.

STAN! STAN! STAN! STAN!

MATTHEWS WAS ALREADY 38 BY THIS STAGE, BUT WOULD GO ON TO PLAY AT THE TOP LEVEL UNTIL HE WAS 50.

HIS REMARKABLE CAREER LONGEVITY COULD BE ATTRIBUTED TO...

ABSTINENCE FROM ALCOHOL AND TOBACCO

WARNING: MAY CAUSE SOPHISTICATION

Suave

FASTING ON MONDAYS

BFC CANTEEN MONDAY SPECIAL! TRIPE

I'll pass.

RUNNING ON THE BEACH IN WEIGHTED SHOES

Lighter shoes or drier sand

STRETCHING EXERCISES

Berlin 1938

Reach, boys!

You don't think people might misinterpret this?

THE MAGICAL MAGYARS
ENGLAND 3 HUNGARY 6, 1953

Hungary's 'Golden Squad' were well drilled for their visit to Wembley in November 1953. They were unbeaten in three years but left nothing to chance. Most of their team played for Honved, so national coach Gusztáv Sebes requested that their club opponents play in an English style to help them prepare. Presumably, the other Hungarian clubs didn't object, as it meant they could just boot the ball out to their wingers and dispense with all that boring 'tactics' nonsense.

Sebes also measured out Hungary's training pitch to the exact dimensions of the one at Wembley and used English footballs. What's more, he watered the pitch and used a smoke machine to replicate the wet and foggy conditions the team could expect on an early winter afternoon in London.

The visitors flew out of the traps but England stood firm, refusing to descend to the level of their swarthy opponents' deceptive use of skill and movement. The Hungarians were running in directions that were, frankly, improper. Their front four tore the English defence to shreds. Nándor Hidegkuti scored a hat-trick as the hosts staggered around in a state of bafflement. That they scored only six was down to their profligacy in front of goal.

The reaction to the 6–3 thrashing in England set the template for future generations, focusing on the need for more passion and decrying the inflated wages of the modern professional, some of whom could afford as many as two baths a week.

Yet this was not to detract from the warmth and appreciation the public felt towards the Hungary team, who were cheered from the pitch and later on to their train at Victoria station. Sebes' pre-match preparation had also instilled within the Hungarians the confidence to use an Oyster card.

HUNGARY ARRIVED AT WEMBLEY IN NOVEMBER 1953 BOASTING A REPUTATION FOR FINE ATTACKING FOOTBALL. ENGLAND, THOUGH, WERE CONFIDENT THAT THEY WOULD PREVAIL THROUGH THE TIME-HONOURED APPLICATION OF SPUNK AND MUSCLE AND VIM AND SPUNK. AS THE TEAMS LINED UP IN THE TUNNEL, THE HOSTS GREW MORE CERTAIN.

This should be easy, lads. Their kit is made of a breathable light-weight material, not like our robust cotton shirts that absorb the London smog. And look at their weird boots! No steel toecaps or ankle restricting wet leather! Feeble.

BUT THEIR NERVE MAY HAVE WAVERED WHEN THEY SAW PUSKÁS CASUALLY JUGGLING THE BALL BEFORE THE KICK OFF.

TIP TAP TAP TIP BOUNCE COMPETENCE

BEFORE ENGLAND HAD EVEN TOUCHED THE BALL IN HUNGARY'S HALF, THE BALL WAS IN THEIR NET. THE INTELLIGENT PASSING AND MOVEMENT OF THE VISITORS BAFFLED ENGLAND. IN PARTICULAR, HIDEGKUTI DROPPING DEEP CAUSED PROBLEMS THEY NEVER SOLVED AND IT WAS HE WHO MADE SPACE FOR HIMSELF AND SMASHED THE BALL INTO THE TOP CORNER.

Time for you to meet 'Bangers' and 'Mash'.

He went... backwards!

HUNGARY SEEMED ABLE TO SCORE AT WILL. MOST MEMORABLY, THEIR THIRD CAME AFTER A FLOWING MOVE ENDED AT THE FEET OF PUSKÁS. HE DRAGGED THE BALL BACK TO AVOID WRIGHT'S DESPERATE LUNGE BEFORE SLAMMING A SHOT IN AT THE NEAR POST; THE HUMILIATION OF THE ENGLAND CAPTAIN ILLUSTRATING THE GULF IN CLASS.

DRAG

HUNGARY WON 6-3, BUT NEVER LET IT BE SAID THAT ENGLAND ARE INCAPABLE OF LEARNING FROM THEIR MISTAKES. COACH WALTER WINTERBOTTOM HATCHED A PLAN FOR THE REMATCH IN BUDAPEST.

The Hungarians think we're too smart to use the same tactics that failed so spectacularly at Wembley, so that's exactly what we'll do. The element of surprise will be the key to success!

HUNGARY WON 7-1. CENTRE-HALF SYD OWEN SAID IT WAS LIKE PLAYING 'PEOPLE FROM OUTER SPACE'.

Isn't he a bit portly for a Cyberman?

PUSKÁS

THE MIRACLE OF BERN
WEST GERMANY 3 HUNGARY 2, 1954

Two weeks before the start of the 1954 World Cup, West Germany's coach Sepp Herberger made his team watch a film of Hungary's 6–3 demolition of England. The players were stunned. Some stared in a catatonic shock, emitting low whining sounds, others sobbed gently. However, these reactions may all have been side-effects of the large doses of supplements the players were routinely injected with. On second viewing, they began to notice some flaws in Hungary's play.

Not that they were able to exploit any of them when the two sides met in the group stage, with Hungary running out 8–3 winners. This transpired to be a cunning trick from Herberger, who had deliberately played a weakened team to lull the Hungarians into a false sense of security. Less subtle was the crunching tackle by Werner Liebrich that left Ferenc Puskás with a hairline fracture of the ankle. Puskás returned to the team later in the tournament but was clearly not fit.

West Germany recovered from the defeat by beating Turkey 7–2. They advanced through the rounds and reached the final via a 6–1 win against Austria. Defending was optional back then. Hungary's progress to the final involved a quarter-final with Brazil, widely considered to be one of the most violent World Cup matches of all time.

Thirty thousand German fans filled the Wankdorf Stadium in Bern for the final and witnessed a spectacular comeback to seal a memorable 3–2 win. The West German national team had re-formed only four years earlier, but now they were crowned world champions. This wasn't to be the first time the *Fußballnationalmannschaft* would benefit from a superior opponent thinking that an early lead in a final was licence to dick about. I'm looking at you, Holland team of 1974.

HUNGARY'S PREPARATIONS FOR THE FINAL WERE FAR FROM IDEAL. ON THE EVE OF THE MATCH THEY WERE KEPT AWAKE BY BRASS BANDS PRACTISING FOR THE SWISS CHAMPIONSHIPS. IT IS BELIEVED THAT THESE ARSEHOLES LATER WENT ON TO RENT THE FLAT ABOVE THE AUTHOR OF THIS BOOK BETWEEN THE YEARS 2010-2014.

Hey, after this we should throw all our saucepans on the laminate flooring and have improbably loud sex!

WHAT'S MORE, NOT ALL OF THE PLAYERS OBSERVED THE CURFEW IMPOSED BY GUSZTÁV SEBES. WINGER ZOLTÁN CZIBOR LATER COMPLAINED ABOUT HAVING TO COVER THE WORK OF AN UN-NAMED PLAYER WHO HE ALLEGED DIDN'T RETURN TO HIS ROOM UNTIL 6AM.

Seriously, I'll be fine once I've had a Sausage McMuffin and a bottle of full-fat Coke. spit

EVEN THE WEATHER WORKED AGAINST THE MAGYARS, WITH THE WET CONDITIONS FAVOURING WEST GERMANY. NONE MORE SO THAN CAPTAIN FRITZ WALTER, WHO WAS FAMED FOR THRIVING IN THE RAIN.

Um, heads or tails?

Sweet, beautiful, life-giving, pass-restricting rain.

ADIDAS FOUNDER ADI DASSLER ALSO PROVIDED THE GERMANS WITH NEW BOOTS, WHICH HELPED THEM TO BETTER COPE WITH THE SODDEN PITCH

This should be easy, lads. Look at their consumerist, branded boots, with their gimmicky screw-in studs that enable them to, um, adapt to variable playing conditions. Dandies!

AFTER EIGHT MINUTES, HUNGARY WERE 2-0 UP, BUT A COMBINATION OF COMPLACENCY AND FATIGUE WAS THEIR UNDOING AND WEST GERMANY FOUGHT BACK TO LEVEL BEFORE HALF-TIME. FIVE MINUTES FROM THE END, HELMUT RAHN GUIDED A LEFT-FOOTED SHOT PAST GROSICS TO WIN THE WORLD CUP.

Really, a mint Cornetto and a little cry, that's all I need.

FOR GERMANS, THE FINAL BECAME KNOWN AS 'THE MIRACLE OF BERN' AND IN 2003 WAS THE SUBJECT OF AN ACTUALLY-QUITE-GOOD FILM. THE PLOT TELLS THE EMOTIONAL STORY OF A BOY AND HIS FATHER WHO TRAVEL TO THE MATCH AND INSPIRE THEIR TEAM TO VICTORY FROM THE SIDELINE.

You can't stand here. Show me your ticket. Yeah, it says here you've got an 'Abominable view' seat. You'll have to get a cable car up to the back of the clock tower. I don't make the rules, mate.

STEWARD

FINAL 1954

IN SUBSEQUENT YEARS, SEPP HERBERGER'S TEAM WOULD FACE ALLEGATIONS OF DOPING, ALL OF WHICH WERE STRENUOUSLY DENIED. FOR THE TIME BEING, THOUGH, THEY WERE HAPPY TO CELEBRATE AS WORLD CHAMPIONS

I'm so happy I could climb into a tyre swing and eat a rival's young.

SCHNA... BONOBO HORROR

ooh

CHAMPION OF CHAMPIONS
THE FORMATION OF THE EUROPEAN CUP

Try to picture a world in which the European Cup was contested purely by the league champions of each country. This bizarre situation can likely be ascribed to the excessive consumption of tinned milk and Marxism. This state of collective lunacy meant that, in 1955, a big rich team could finish third or fourth in their league and miss out on the chance to add to their vast wealth.

For decades, attempts had been made to organise a competition for Europe's best clubs. As far back as 1897 there had been a challenge cup for teams from the Austro-Hungarian Empire. It was succeeded by competitions like the Mitropa Cup – the brainchild of Austria's famous coach Hugo Meisl, who may have come up with the idea over a cronut down at the Ring Café.

Europe had settled down a bit after the Second World War and commercial air travel was becoming more accessible. Floodlit international club friendlies became more common. One such friendly saw the famous Honved team from Hungary facing Wolverhampton Wanderers in December 1954. Wolves won 3–2, leading to wild declarations of supremacy in the British press. This frustrated Gabriel Hanot, the editor of French sports newspaper *L'Équipe*. Hanot had long proposed a European-wide tournament and he took his suggestion to the newly-formed UEFA. After a bit of regulation bickering with FIFA over who would run the competition, it was agreed that the first European Cup would kick off during the 1955–56 season.

For the first season only, *L'Équipe* was tasked with selecting the competitors on the basis of which clubs they found to be the most representative or prestigious – a model that Europe's big clubs would support enthusiastically today. The typically progressive football authorities in England banned their teams from entering, which meant Chelsea missed out. Wolves, unofficial champions of the universe, weren't asked at all. Rude.

L'EQUIPE OFFICES - 1954

Have you seen this? De gaulle of it!

Indeed. It's a pity that the English football authorities don't share the same enthusiasm for international contests...

WOLVES - CHAMPIONS OF THE WORLD!

Experts say jumping to conclusions based on limited evidence the best way to decide.

LONDON

We've been invited to participate in a multi-national—

Oh, yeah, that's the same week as the Kent FA's annual jam carnival, so y'know...

What's needed is a pan-European competition to decide the real champion.

What about the Mitropa Cup?

A fine competition, but limited to Eastern and Central Europe. In time it will become marginalised and competed for purely by obscure lower league clubs...

Now this is more like it.

History tells us there is an appetite for such a club tournament. Remember the Coupe des Nations in 1930? That was hugely successful, despite clashing with the World Cup.

MONTEVIDEO - 1930

It's been a triumph. If only more Europeans had participated though.

Oh yeah, they're doing their own thing in Geneva. They've got blue-chip sponsors and lucrative radiogram broadcast deals. It sounds awesome.

Yep, the Gazprom will be flowing there all right. Anyway, when does our two-week boat trip to France depart?

The infrastructure is now in place for this to happen. We have safe, affordable air travel; efficient 60 watt floodlights and peace in Europe (if you discount the atmosphere of open hostility between the two sides of the continent).

We'll put it to UEFA and then it will just be a straightforward matter of inviting the teams.

We've been—

No.

THE BOYS FROM BRAZIL
BRAZIL WIN THE 1958 WORLD CUP

Brazil arrived at the 1958 World Cup carrying the mental pain of their defeat at home in 1950 and the physical pain of a violent elimination to Hungary in 1954. But this was to be their time. Coached by the avuncular Vicente Feola, a large man prone to nodding off during training sessions (dribble round this, shoot at that; who wouldn't need a power nap after watching a few thousand of those?), Brazil swept all before them.

Didi, who had almost been omitted from the World Cup squad, was voted player of the tournament, while Garrincha and Pelé emerged as world stars. Brazil would never lose when they were both in the side.

At the tournament's conclusion, when the captain, Bellini, was presented with the trophy, the mass of cameramen complained that they couldn't see it, so he raised the cup above his head. Lifting trophies in that way would become traditional, be they World Cups or Zenith Data Systems Cups or just objects you've pilfered from the pub.

Another precedent was set by Pelé's club, Santos. Realising they had a bankable asset within their ranks, they embarked upon a world tour in 1959. That year Pelé played more than 100 games, including a fifteen-week tour of Europe. *Joga bonito*!

HAVING BEEN BURNT BY PREVIOUS FAILURES, BRAZIL LEFT NOTHING TO CHANCE FOR THE 1958 WORLD CUP. THEIR METICULOUS PREPARATIONS EVEN EXTENDED TO ORAL HEALTHCARE, WITH A DENTIST EMPLOYED TO REMOVE 470 TEETH FROM 33 PLAYERS.

Is it safe?

What? I don't know! They don't tell me anything, man. I'm only the left-back!

Is it safe?

AND IN AN ATTEMPT TO KEEP THE SQUAD FOCUSED, THE FEMALE WORKERS AT THEIR HOTEL WERE REPLACED WITH MEN AND A LOCAL NUDIST COLONY WAS CLOSED.

If organised religion has taught us anything it's that enforced celibacy never causes problems.

Yes, and demonising women is fine if it is for the greater good.

Begone foul temptresses!

COACH VICENTE FEOLA ALSO EMPLOYED A PSYCHOLOGIST WHOSE REGULAR JOB INVOLVED ASSESSING THE SUITABILITY OF PEOPLE APPLYING TO BE BUS DRIVERS.

I asked the subjects to produce a drawing. Pelé's was particularly disappointing. He chose to draw a lengthy marketing plan outlining future advertising revenue. He didn't even draw a bus.

Global tour → Break America → Still erectile dysfunction drugs!! ($)

And what about Garrincha?

Hmm. The less said about that the better...

Ok, let's re-open that nudist camp.

Yep.

PELÉ AND GARRINCHA WERE OMITTED FROM THE FIRST TWO GAMES, BUT ONCE THEY WERE RECALLED THEY HELPED INSPIRE BRAZIL THROUGH TO A FINAL WITH HOSTS SWEDEN. BUT PANIC STRUCK WHEN THEY REALISED THEY WOULD BE UNABLE TO WEAR THEIR LUCKY YELLOW SHIRTS, SO SOMEONE WAS DESPATCHED TO A LOCAL SPORTS SHOP TO BUY A SET OF BLUE KITS.

Ok, we can do you a deal on these, but we want a say in team selection and you'll have to undertake a year-long tour to promote our brand.

BR

BRAZIL RAN OUT 5-2 WINNERS, WITH THE PICK OF THE GOALS COMING FROM THE 17-YEAR OLD PELÉ. A STAR WAS BORN, AND AT THE END OF THE MATCH, THE EMOTIONALLY EXHAUSTED TEENAGER COLLAPSED INTO THE ARMS OF GOALKEEPER GILMAR.

It's ok, Edson.

Shh, don't move. I can use this image for the Viagra ad campaign.

FIVE IN A ROW
REAL MADRID'S EUROPEAN DOMINATION

Real Madrid won the first five European Cups, their most memorable being the last of the bunch: a 7–3 victory against Eintracht Frankfurt in front of 127,000 people at Hampden Park, Glasgow, in 1960.

Real's president Santiago Bernabéu had overseen a complete change of the club's fortunes. When he was appointed to the role in 1943, they were playing in a ramshackle stadium and didn't even offer group tours and luncheon packages. By the time of his departure, the stadium – renamed in his honour – had been transformed into a cavernous bowl and the team was one of the most feared in Europe.

Bernabéu also forged close relationships with the Franco dictatorship, which led to the occasional act of assistance, such as the granting of special permits to allow sports cars to be imported for star players. In the 1950s, their fame was spread through the new medium of television, the output of which was strictly controlled by the regime. Real Madrid matches were frequently televised, helping to grow their popularity.

But the most crucial intervention was the one that assisted their capture of Alberto Di Stéfano. The team included many greats but it was Di Stéfano who was the most dominant, both on and off the pitch. Even Puskás knew his place. When Real Madrid signed the Hungarian legend, the press dubbed him 'The Little Cannon'. Di Stéfano preferred to call him 'The Big Gut', proving yet again that workplace bullying gets results. The two gelled perfectly on the pitch, though, never more so than in the thrashing of poor old Frankfurt.

REAL MADRID AND BARCELONA HOOVERING UP THE WORLD'S BEST FOOTBALL TALENT ISN'T A NEW PHENOMENON. IN 1953 THEY WERE BATTLING OVER WHO WOULD CAPTURE THE ARGENTINE FORWARD ALFREDO DI STÉFANO.

THE SPANISH FOOTBALL FEDERATION DECREED THAT HE SHOULD PLAY ALTERNATE SEASONS FOR EACH CLUB. HOWEVER, AFTER A POOR START AT MADRID, BARCA DECIDED THEY COULD KEEP HIM. HE WOULD GO ON TO BECOME THE MOST IMPORTANT PLAYER IN REAL'S HISTORY, OUTPERFORMING ALL OTHER GREATS IN THEIR PANTHEON OF LEGENDS.

YES, EVEN

JONATHAN WOODGATE

THE WEST GERMAN FA HAD BANNED ALL ITS CLUBS FROM PLAYING ANY TEAM CONTAINING FERENC PUSKÁS, FURIOUS AT HIS ALLEGATIONS OF DOPING AFTER THE 1954 WORLD CUP FINAL. PUSKÁS HAD TO OFFER A FULL APOLOGY IN ORDER FOR FRANKFURT TO BE ALLOWED TO FACE REAL MADRID.

I'm sooo, sooo, sorry...

AFTER A CAUTIOUS OPENING 20 MINUTES, RICHARD KRESS GAVE EINTRACHT FRANKFURT A SURPRISE LEAD.

BUT THIS SERVED MERELY TO PROVOKE MADRID INTO ACTION.

Nice goal, Richard. Now all we need to do is...

'...keep things...'

1-1

'...tight at...'

2-1

'...the back...'

3-1

'...and hold...'

4-1

'...out for a...'

5-1

'...shock win...'

6-1

ERWIN STEIN PULLED ONE BACK FOR FRANKFURT, BUT STRAIGHT FROM THE KICK-OFF DI STÉFANO CHARGED DOWN THE MIDDLE AND FIRED IN A SEVENTH. STEIN ADDED ANOTHER SOON AFTER TO COMPLETE THE SCORING.

Nice goal, Erwin. Now all we need to do is...

Shut up.

7-3

MADRID'S DOMINANCE OF THE CUP CAME TO AN END THE FOLLOWING SEASON WHEN THEY WERE ELIMINATED IN THE FIRST ROUND BY BARCELONA. ENGLISH REFEREE REG LEAFE DISALLOWED THREE MADRID GOALS AND WAS SURROUNDED BY ANGRY PLAYERS AT THE POST-MATCH BANQUET. THE FACT THAT HE EVEN ATTENDED WAS TESTAMENT TO THE LENGTHS BRITISH PEOPLE WILL GO FOR A BUFFET.

Ooh, scotch eggs...

DELAUNEY'S VISION REALISED
THE FIRST EUROPEAN FOOTBALL CHAMPIONSHIPS

The 1957 UEFA Congress wasn't overwhelmed with enthusiasm at the prospect of a European Nations' Cup. After all, there were other leisure pursuits to be enjoyed during the long European summers of the 1950s, such as holiday camps, bingo and the perennial favourite: violent suppression of political dissidents. Despite several big nations either abstaining or voting against it, the motion was passed for a tournament to begin the next year.

The inaugural tournament was held in France and consisted of four teams: USSR, Yugoslavia, Czechoslovakia and France. Seventeen teams had participated in the qualifying rounds but there were some notable absentees, including West Germany, Italy and England (of *course* England. Anyone would think the English have an innate inclination to say 'nah, you're all right, thanks' in almost any given circumstance). It had taken a flurry of late entrants to get enough teams together to make the competition viable.

The trophy was named in honour of Henri Delaunay, the former UEFA general secretary who had long campaigned for a European Nations' Cup. He had died three years before the start of the competition, so missed the spectacle of 100,000 people watching the first match at Moscow's Central Lenin Stadium. The Soviet Union ran out 3–1 winners against Hungary, sending their fans home marginally less miserable.

THE IDEA OF A EUROPEAN NATIONS CUP WAS FIRST PROPOSED BY HENRI DELAUNAY IN 1927, BUT IT WASN'T UNTIL AFTER THE SECOND WORLD WAR - ONCE EVERYONE WAS FRIENDS AGAIN - THAT THE IDEA GOT OFF THE GROUND.

They're discussing the idea of a European football tournament, General.

Glamour ties with Europe's elite are fine, but our bread and butter is British Home Internationals in front of 4,000 hardy souls at The Racecourse Ground, so...

Hahahahaha!

Sorry.

THE FIRST TOURNAMENT TOOK PLACE IN 1960. SPAIN WITH-DREW AT THE QUALIFYING STAGE AFTER GENERAL FRANCO REFUSED TO LET THE TEAM PLAY THE USSR.

Those Stalinist pigs will be furious when they realise that I've...um, effectively given them a bye to the finals. I wish I could see their stupid faces! Ah haha.

FRANCO'S HATRED OF COMMUNISTS EXTENDED TO HIM QUESTIONING SPANISH CLUB PLAYERS UPON THEIR RETURN FROM EUROPEAN TIES BEHIND THE IRON CURTAIN. HE PARTICULARLY LIKED HEARING STORIES OF POVERTY AND SUFFERING.

Tell me again how they can't even get Levis jeans and have to eat their neighbours' cats!

FRANCO WAS A BIT OF A DICK.

THE USSR WON THROUGH TO THE FINAL IN PARIS, WHERE THEY FACED YUGOSLAVIA IN THE OUT-OF-DATE ATLAS DERBY.

Give it time.

THE SOVIET UNION WERE BOLSTERED BY THE PRESENCE OF LEGENDARY GOALKEEPER **LEV YASHIN**, WHOSE ADVICE TO THOSE SEEKING TO EMULATE HIS SUCCESS WAS TO:

Have a quick smoke to calm your nerves, then toss back a strong drink to tone your muscles.

ON AN UNRELATED MEDICAL NOTE, YASHIN SUFFERED FROM A GASTRIC ULCER HIS ENTIRE ADULT LIFE.

YUGOSLAVIA DOMINATED AND LED THROUGH MILAN GALIĆ'S DEFLECTED SHOT, BUT A MISTAKE FROM THEIR GOALKEEPER VIDINIĆ ALLOWED METREVELI TO EQUALISE.

I knew I should have got more drunk.

A VIKTOR PONEDELNIK GOAL WON THE CUP FOR THE USSR LATE IN EXTRA-TIME. AT THE FINAL WHISTLE, LEV YASHIN'S FAMOUS CAP WAS STOLEN IN A PITCH INVASION.

C'est un grand souvenir!

urgh...

ULCER B-GONE

FIGHT THE POWER
THE ABOLITION OF THE MAXIMUM WAGE

I know what you're thinking: 'They should give soldiers the same salaries as footballers, even though the footballers who play in the lower leagues earn less than people in the higher-ranking military positions. Also, all footballers should be made to ring every person in the country and *personally explain* to them why they preferred to spend their two-week off-season enjoying a family holiday at Disneyland, rather than orchestrating drone strikes against Isis.'

The issue of footballers' wages has always been contentious, from the early days of professionalism through to the present era of players driving cars the size of houses and living in houses the size of Ipswich. But for years players were forced to work in restrictive employment conditions; the maximum wage and 'retain and transfer' system being the two major impediments to a footballer working where he wanted and earning enough money from a short career.

Eventually, the players organised and defeated the football authorities and powerful club owners. These empowering victories led us to the present situation whereby most players couldn't even point out Helmand Province on an atlas, let alone do a tour of duty there to protect the economic and mineral interests of successive governments.

AS WE KNOW, THE MODERN DAY ELITE FOOTBALLER IS ABLE TO EARN VAST QUANTITIES OF CASH THROUGHOUT THE COURSE OF A CAREER...

Ooh, the moon's a funny colour tonight.

Yeah, Micah Richards has bought it and is using the surface as a storage space for all his gold. He's filled Saturn with his spare cars.

BUT IT WASN'T ALWAYS THIS WAY...

THE FOOTBALL AUTHORITIES RELUCTANTLY AGREED TO PROFESSIONALISM IN 1885. DARWEN FC HAD BECOME THE FIRST CLUB TO PAY THEIR PLAYERS IN 1879, CAUSING CONSTERNATION IN SOME QUARTERS.

How many shillings a week?! Dear Lord, your financial recklessness knows no bounds!

HE WAS RIGHT, DARWEN WOULD GO BUST JUST 130 YEARS LATER.

THE FOOTBALL LEAGUE INTRODUCED A MAXIMUM WAGE OF £4 A WEEK IN 1901. BONUS PAYMENTS WERE ALSO BANNED. AS MOST PLAYERS DIDN'T EARN MUCH, THERE WAS LITTLE PROTEST – AN ATTITUDE TO MONEY THAT ENDURES TO THIS DAY.

No, I couldn't possibly accept a pay rise. I am already handsomely remunerated.

THE MAXIMUM WAGE ROSE OVER THE YEARS, BUT MANY PLAYERS STILL HAD TO TAKE PAID EMPLOYMENT OUTSIDE OF FOOTBALL TO GET BY. CLUBS ALSO FOUND WAYS OF CIRCUMNAVIGATING THE RULES, WITH SOME PLAYERS GIVEN JOBS AT COMPANIES OWNED BY CLUB DIRECTORS AS A WAY OF SUPPLEMENTING THEIR INCOME.

Guys, let's imagineer a roadmap to synergy, yeah

FLUX
TRACTION
VALUE ADD
TAPESTRY OF INNOVATION

Christ.

THE 'RETAIN AND TRANSFER' SYSTEM ALSO MEANT THAT PLAYERS COULD NOT MOVE WITHOUT THE PERMISSION OF THE CLUB, EVEN WHEN THEIR CONTRACT HAD EXPIRED

CHAIRMAN

Let you go?! No way, we'll need those long bony fingers down at my pie factory when the squirrel shredder gets clogged with fur.

IT WASN'T UNTIL 1961 THAT THE MAXIMUM WAGE WAS ABOLISHED. THIS WAS LARGELY DOWN TO THE INTERVENTION OF THE PFA CHAIRMAN, JIMMY HILL, AND THE VERY REAL THREAT OF STRIKE ACTION.

DAYS AFTER THE REMOVAL OF THE SALARY CAP, HILL'S FULHAM TEAM-MATE, JOHNNY HAYNES, BECAME BRITAIN'S FIRST £100-A-WEEK PLAYER. THUS, FOOTBALL'S BLING CULTURE WAS BORN.

This is why I'm hot, this is why I'm hot. I'm hot coz air conditioning isn't standard in cars yet.

COTTAGR

BOUNCE BOUNCE

Wow! Teak panelling, brass wheel rims and a rad beige paint job!

THE BATTLE OF SANTIAGO
CHILE v ITALY, 1962

Let's get one thing clear from the outset: absolutely no one loves to see an international grudge match with a simmering political subtext descend into a series of scraps, fist fights and flying karate kicks. Indeed, there is no amusement that can be derived from seeing grown adults publicly losing it in a spectacular fashion. The publishers of this book would discourage anyone from immediately typing 'The Battle of Santiago' into a search engine, plumping up the cushions nice and soft and watching the ensuing three minutes and fifty-four seconds of comedy dynamite. Strict parental guidance should be exercised to ensure that no children see the video, as they definitely wouldn't find it great fun either.

Chile v Italy in the group stage of the 1962 World Cup didn't stand out as a fixture that had the potential for disorder. The two nations had never previously met on the football field and had no significant relationship of which to speak, but some ill-chosen words in the build-up to the match led to one of the most infamous bust-ups in World Cup history.

English referee Ken Aston had the task of keeping order. He comprehensively failed to achieve that but you do have to have some sympathy. 'I wasn't reffing a football match, I was acting as an umpire in military manoeuvres,' he later said. Perhaps as a result of this experience, Aston was subsequently credited with the invention of red and yellow cards.

On the BBC, a furious David Coleman introduced the highlights package...

Good evening. The game you are about to see is the most stupid, appalling, disgusting and disgraceful exhibition...

CHILEAN BLOOD WAS ALREADY BOILING AFTER LOCAL NEWSPAPERS RE-PUBLISHED THE STORIES OF TWO ITALIAN JOURNALISTS WHO HAD PENNED SCATHING OBSERVATIONS ON LIFE IN SANTIAGO.

THEY WERE FORCED TO FLEE THE COUNTRY, WHILE AN ARGENTINIAN JOURNALIST WAS ROUGHED UP, THE VICTIM OF MISTAKEN IDENTITY.

They say our phones don't work, our streets are full of sex workers and that taxis are as rare as faithful husbands! Gather the boys, we need to form an angry mob.

PERIODICO INSOLTOS ITALIANI

It's broken.

Give us a one-star review on Trip Advisor, will you?

THIS SET THE TONE FOR THE MATCH, WITH CHAOS REIGNING FROM THE FIRST WHISTLE. AMONG OTHER INCIDENTS...

ITALY'S FERRINI WAS SENT OFF FOR TAKING OUT LEONEL SÁNCHEZ AFTER JUST SEVEN MINUTES. HE REFUSED TO GO QUIETLY AND WAS DRAGGED OFF THE PITCH BY A TROOP OF UNIFORMED MEN.

The Chilean military is friendly, right? ... Guys?

IN THE ENSUING SCRAP, SOMEONE BROKE HUMBERTO MASCHIO'S NOSE.

SOON AFTER, MARIO DAVID AIMED A FEW WILD HACKS AT A FLOORED SÁNCHEZ. THE CHILEAN - WHOSE FATHER WAS A BOXER-RESPONDED WITH A SHARP LEFT HOOK. REFEREE KEN ASTON TAKES NO ACTION.

DAVID LATER TOOK REVENGE WITH A FLYING, HEAD-HEIGHT KICK ON SÁNCHEZ.

HOWEVER, HE SNUCK BACK ON TO THE PITCH AND BRIEFLY RETOOK HIS PLACE IN THE ITALIAN DEFENCE.

Oi!

wuh?

THE GAME CARRIED ON IN THIS FASHION, BUT CHILE SCORED TWO LATE GOALS AND ITALY WERE KNOCKED OUT.

SÁNCHEZ AND DAVID LATER WENT ON TO PLAY TOGETHER AT AC MILAN.

WHO AMONG US CAN SAY THAT, AT SOME POINT, THEY HAVEN'T WANTED TO AIM A FLYING KICK AT A COLLEAGUE?

I'm not being racist, but...

THE LITTLE BIRD
TAKES FLIGHT
BRAZIL RETAIN THE WORLD CUP, 1962

World champions Brazil retained their title with almost the same team as four years previously. They were now coached by Aymoré Moreira, who had taken over when Feola fell ill.

Pelé, by now twenty-one and globally famous, lasted only two matches but was replaced by Amarildo, who was exceptional once he'd emerged from his shell (you kept the receipt for this book, right?).

As in 1954, they conceded the first goal in the final; European Footballer of the Year Josef Masopust giving Czechoslovakia the lead with a quickly taken shot. Brazil soon recovered, though, with an equaliser from Amarildo showing them the way (seriously, they have to give you a refund, or at least an exchange for a similarly priced item). Zito and Vavá added second-half goals to complete a 3–1 win.

AS IN 1958, BRAZIL'S PREPARATIONS WERE METICULOUS, WITH DELEGATES FROM THEIR TECHNICAL COMMISSION EVEN TAKING THE TIME TO INSPECT THE LOCAL, GOVERNMENT-LICENCED BROTHELS.

Those Italians said this whole country is one big bordello, so we're going to have our work cut out!

Right, that's it...

Leave it, Dave!

PELÉ WAS INJURED EARLY ON, BUT THE TOURNAMENT BELONGED TO GARRINCHA. NICKNAMED 'THE LITTLE BIRD', HE'D OVERCOME PHYSICAL BIRTH DEFECTS TO BECOME ONE OF THE GAME'S GREATS.

HE DESTROYED ENGLAND IN THE QUARTER-FINALS, SCORING TWO FINE GOALS AND CREATING CONSTANT HAVOC. IN THE SECOND HALF, A SMALL DOG RAN ON TO THE PITCH. IT EVADED GARRINCHA, BUT WAS SCOOPED UP BY JIMMY GREAVES.

Well the day hasn't been a complete disaster...

GARRINCHA LATER ADOPTED THE DOG AND NAMED IT 'GREAVSIE'. IT WENT ON TO PRESENT A POPULAR SATURDAY LUNCHTIME TV SHOW IN THE U.K.

Rottish roal reepers are rurrish

HAHAHAHAHAHAHAHA!!

You slay me, Greavsie.

GARRINCHA SCORED ANOTHER TWO IN THE SEMI-FINAL AGAINST CHILE, BUT WAS SENT OFF AFTER KNEEING A DEFENDER UP THE ARSE; SOMETHING THE TEAM PSYCHOLOGIST PROBABLY HADN'T ACCOUNTED FOR.

My analysis shows he has zero aggression, but his slapstick readings are off the charts.

But what can it mean?

CHAPLINGRAPH READING

AS HE TRAIPSED TO THE STANDS, THE HOME CROWD TREATED HIM TO A TRADITIONAL CHILEAN FAREWELL.

HE FACED THE PROSPECT OF MISSING THE FINAL, BUT BRAZIL MANAGED TO GET HIS SUSPENSION OVERTURNED. THE LINESMAN WHO'D SEEN THE INCIDENT MYSTERIOUSLY LEFT CHILE THE NEXT MORNING.

Oh stop complaining. There are worse ways to be disappeared you know.

GARRINCHA WAS STRANGELY SUBDUED IN THE FINAL — ALMOST AS IF HE WAS RECOVERING FROM A RECENT HEAD INJURY. STILL, BRAZIL CAME FROM BEHIND TO BEAT CZECHOSLOVAKIA 3-1, WITH GOALS FROM AMARILDO, ZITO AND VAVÁ.

I don't know how many more happy endings I can take.

FOLLOW THAT STAR
THE BIRTH OF JOSÉ MOURINHO

José Mário dos Santos Mourinho Félix was born in Setúbal, near Lisbon, on 26 January 1963, aged forty-five.

José was from humble stock. His mother was a primary school teacher, his father a decent footballer who even made a solitary appearance for Portugal. Who could have guessed that this unremarkable middle-class couple would produce the saviour of pragmatic, scowl-based football?

Whether he was poking his finger in an opposition coach's eye, laughing sarcastically into the face of a fourth official, undermining a colleague for doing her job, or merely blaming his own failings on a cabal of dithering ballboys, José taught us never to turn our cheeks to even the most imperceptible of slights.

That he was able to achieve all of this while being completely one-eyed is testament to a youthful exuberance, which could almost be described as childish. The world all wept as he was betrayed by the one they call Eden Hazard. Our only recourse was to scrawl abstract felt-tip messages on to soiled bedsheets. As Chelsea flirted with relegation in the early part of the 2015–16 season, tears rolled down the cheeks of football fans everywhere.

But rejoice, for José is risen, his career resurrected at Manchester United (where he will do well in his first couple of seasons before alienating everyone and getting fired in his third season).

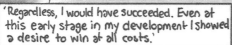

FLIGHT OF THE CHOLLIMA
NORTH KOREA, 1966

Little was expected of North Korea at the 1966 World Cup. They'd qualified by beating Australia in a play-off but all the other teams in Asia, Oceania and Africa had withdrawn in protest at being allocated only one qualification spot between them. FIFA wasn't the shining paragon of progressiveness we know today.

Even getting into England for the tournament was problematic. There was no diplomatic relationship between Great Britain and North Korea and the Foreign Office reluctantly gave them entry clearance on the strict proviso that they never be referred to as the Democratic People's Republic of Korea. It was also ruled that no national anthems be played at the whole tournament, apart from before the opening match and the final, which they banked on North Korea not making. Is a World Cup even worthy of the name if it doesn't include close-ups of tearful footballers singing off-key renditions of pointless songs about mountains and seas and dead kings?

Their chances looked even slimmer after being drawn in a tough group with the Soviet Union, Chile and, fatefully, Italy. *The Times* wrote: 'Unless the Koreans turn out to be jugglers, with some unexpected ploy like running with the ball cushioned in the crook of their necks, it looks as though Italy and Russia should have the run of the place'.

However, they drew strength from their team nickname of *Chollima*, a mythical winged horse that cannot be mounted by a mortal man. For a brief time in June '66, they soared high above England's green hills, whence they crapped all over the heads of some Italian footballers.

THEY THINK IT'S ALL OVER...
ENGLAND WIN THE 1966 WORLD CUP

The England team. A great source of national pride. Whether they are battling to a goalless draw with Costa Rica or bravely capitulating to Iceland, this group of terrified men so often act as a great unifier; the collective groans that their performances inspire spanning all social and political divides. Rich or poor; young or old; black or white; we all come together every two years to wonder how professional footballers are incapable of taking a set-piece that clears the first man.

Their brand of football has become familiar, almost predictable; and, like all the best teams in the world, it is played to a distinctive rhythm. The Brazilians have the samba drums; the Spanish, the confident steps of the flamenco dancer; Germany, the technically pristine coordination of synth-pop. England play to the beat of six sunburnt blokes in plastic bowler hats farting 'God Save the Queen' through dented brass instruments. As such, their football boasts the fluidity of a bowl of congealed custard at a royal wedding street party. This is England's DNA. If you were emotionally capable, you would cry.

However, there was a brief sliver of time when England's misplaced sense of entitlement was justified: 1988, when Bryan Robson lifted The Rous Cup in front of 25,756 ecstatic fans at Wembley. But also, before that, 1966.

Much like the endless stream of Hitler documentaries on The History Channel, there are few angles on England's 1966 World Cup win left unexplored (e.g. 'George Cohen's Secret Dinosaur Army', 'Pickles Tunnel to the Underworld', 'The Hunt for Roger Hunt' etc.). The facts of the story are so well known, but with another page to fill for the sake of the book layout, they are worth repeating.

England got off to a typically slow start, with a drab goalless draw against Uruguay. Results improved in their remaining group matches, with 2-0 wins against Mexico and France, but the performances were still incoherent. England's second goal against France had come moments after Nobby Stiles had committed a brutal foul on Jacques Simon that went unpunished. This was the first of the handful of incidents at the World Cup that led some to believe that England's triumph was pre-ordained.

FIFA warned Stiles about his future conduct and the FA asked manager Alf Ramsey whether it was entirely necessary to have him in the side. Ramsey threatened to resign and the blazers backed off. Alf wasn't a man to mess with.

The quarter-final victory against Argentina is best-remembered for the sending off of their captain, Antonio Rattin and the furore that followed. Rattin had collected an early booking for a lunge on Bobby Charlton, and after being penalised in the 36th minute for another foul on Hurst, he ranted at the referee, Rudolf Kreitlin, until the German's patience snapped and he sent him off. Confusion reigned, as Rattin initially refused to leave the field, requesting the services of a translator to clarify that he was merely commending the referee on an exemplary performance and unquestionable parentage. Eventually, he relented and took a long, forlorn walk around the edge of the pitch; a translator not being required to interpret the heckles of the Wembley crowd.

The match was settled with a late header from Geoff Hurst. Upon the final whistle, Ramsey attempted to stop his players from swapping shirts with the South Americans and later compared them to animals. A small boy ran on to the pitch to celebrate, Argentina's Oscar Más clipped him round the ear. This old school, low-level child abuse may seem harmless until you discover that the child grew up to be Nigel Farage, probably.

Popular myth has it that England's semi-final was moved from Goodison Park to Wembley, but this was never the case. The FA had uncharacteristically jumped the gun and instructed the press that the game would be played in Liverpool. However, FIFA had always said that the allocation of the venues would only be made after the semi-finalists were known.

Finally, England put in a performance worthy of world champions. Two goals from Bobby Charlton put them in control, but then his brother Jack punched a shot off the line (no red card? What a stitch-up!), allowing Eusébio to pull one back from the spot. The hosts held on and advanced to the final with West Germany and a famous victory that would put them on the irrevocable path to appointing Sam Allardyce as manager.

1966 TRUTHERS BELIEVE THAT ENGLAND BENEFITED FROM A NUMBER OF CONSPIRACIES TO WIN THE WORLD CUP.

THE STOLEN TROPHY

THE CHANGE OF THE VENUE FOR THE SEMI-FINAL

GEOFF HURST'S SECOND GOAL

THE CLEAR HANDBALL IN THE BUILD UP TO WEST GERMANY'S LATE EQUALISER.

Well, they couldn't make it OBVIOUS.

Pickles 'the dog' found the trophy just 10 miles from MI5 HQ. Fishy.

The blazered Lizard Men moved England's semi-final to Wembley so more lizard people could see it.

Jet fuel can't melt crossbars, people!

BUT THE SIMPLE FACT IS THAT, FOR ONCE, ENGLAND WERE THE BEST TEAM IN THE WORLD.

THE NATION WAS ABUZZ AS THE TEAM ADVANCED THROUGH THE COMPETITION, EVEN TURNING A BLIND EYE TO THE FACT THAT THE TOURNAMENT MASCOT LOOKED LIKE A RIGHT-WING CANDIDATE IN THE BROMLEY BY-ELECTION.

You're not even allowed to call it Christmas any more.

WORLD CUP

LONDON IN THE MID-SIXTIES WAS A FREE-SPIRITED, SWINGING TOWN AND NO ONE EPITOMISED THIS GROOVY SPIRIT MORE THAN ENGLAND MANAGER ALF RAMSEY.

We've done it! We're world champions, Alf!

Sit down and behave yourself, man.

RAMSEY WAS A MASTER TACTICIAN BUT DIPLOMACY WASN'T HIS STRONG POINT. AFTER A BAD-TEMPERED QUARTER-FINAL WITH ARGENTINA, HE OUTRAGED THE SOUTH AMERICANS BY LIKENING THEM TO ANIMALS.

Yeah, you bloody tell 'em, Alf; sub-human, the lot of 'em.

Well, I didn't mean it like that...

Good for you, Alf; good for you.

HOWEVER, HIS SINGLE-MINDEDNESS SAW HIM WRESTLE TEAM SELECTION AWAY FROM THE FA AND MEANT HE WAS ABLE TO RESIST THEIR CALLS TO DROP THE COMBATIVE MIDFIELDER NOBBY STILES AFTER A SLOW START.

ENGLAND REMAINS AT THE CENTRE OF THE FOOTBALL UNIVERSE, SO EVERYONE IS FAMILIAR WITH THE STORY OF THE '66 FINAL.

ITALIA

NIGERIA

HURST'S HAT-TRICK, THE QUEEN'S GLOVES, RAMSEY TELLING A WAITER AT THE POST-MATCH BANQUET: 'I DON'T WANT NO FUCKING PEAS'; LEGENDS ALL.

THE PIVOTAL MOMENT CAME IN THE 100TH MINUTE WHEN THE AZERBAIJANI LINESMAN, TOFIK BAKHRAMOV, RULED THAT HURST'S SHOT HAD CROSSED THE LINE, PUTTING ENGLAND 3-2 UP. WHEN A STATUE OF BAKHRAMOV WAS UNVEILED IN HIS HOMELAND IN 2004, GEOFF HURST WAS A GUEST OF HONOUR.

CONSPIRACY!!

BUT THINGS COULD HAVE BEEN VERY DIFFERENT HAD THE GOAL BEEN DISALLOWED...

Hurst can he do it? Yes! Yes he has done!

No, no. The linesman says no. No goal.

England are furious, but the Germans break and it's HELD! He's won the World Cup for West Germany!

Her Majesty the Queen there, maintaining a dignified stoicism.

TOR!

And some people are on the pitch ...they've noticed the Queen's reaction and are questioning the relevance of the monarchy in a modern society.

The money we spend on this redundant institution could fund handkerchief hats for all! SMASH THE SYSTEM!!

And they've turned Buckingham Palace into a toy brick fun park, increasing tourism revenue.

And in the spirit of change, Alf Ramsey visits Argentina to apologise for his rudeness, forging a lasting friendship between the two nations.

Sorry about all that

Please, don't mention it, friend.

LET'S NEVER FIGHT AGAIN

And while he's there, he relaxes, ditches the elocution lessons, grows some sideburns and learns to love maverick players.

Ziggy plays left mid, linking good with Bowles and Currie.

And England's new possession-based team, built upon the principles of skill and freedom of expression dominates world football for generations to come.

No, wait, the linesman has given the goal after all.

Thank God for that. The after-dinner speaking circuit is congested as it is.

THE LISBON LIONS
CELTIC 2 INTER 1, 1967

On a sun-drenched evening in Lisbon in 1967, Celtic became the first British team, and the only Scottish team, to win the European Cup. Jock Stein's squad of local players overcame the revered Inter team, flooring them with a performance of dogged attacking verve.

Inter had won two of the three previous finals and were clear favourites, but their season was collapsing around them. They had been knocked out of the Coppa Italia and were in the middle of a slump that would see them lose the Scudetto to Juventus. Celtic, meanwhile, came into the final having won the league, the Scottish Cup and the Scottish League Cup.

The Inter players' nerves were shredded further by the insistence of their coach, Helenio Herrera, on cutting them off from the outside world for extended periods of time. For the final, he booked an entire hotel for the exclusive use of the players and coaching staff; even club officials were barred. Spending that much time confined to a hotel would drive anyone mad and it perhaps wasn't long before they were amusing themselves by making Alan Partridge-style zombie outfits from shower curtains and tungsten-tipped screws.

Some had dismissed Celtic's win as a fluke, but a week later Stein's Lisbon Lions beat Real Madrid 1–0 in Di Stéfano's testimonial match, cementing their status as the champions of Europe. Perhaps even a few Rangers fans allowed themselves a wry smile as they ripped their television sets from the wall, smashing them into a thousand pieces on their living room carpet.

THAT NIGHT
IN NORTH LONDON
MANCHESTER UNITED WIN
THE EUROPEAN CUP, 1968

Manchester United's victory in the 1968 European Cup final was the culmination of a story of recovery ten years in the making. In 1958, eight of their players had perished in the Munich air disaster, which claimed twenty-three lives in total. Manager Matt Busby was seriously injured in the crash but recovered to rebuild a team that would eventually become champions of Europe.

United goalkeeper Alex Stepney said that no one ever spoke of Munich but there were two players in the team who survived the disaster: Bill Foulkes and Bobby Charlton.

Stepney would play a key part in the final, denying Eusébio with a late save when the scores were deadlocked. Eusébio, the great sportsman, applauded his opponent, while his Benfica team-mates silently looked on. What could you say; it was bloody Eusébio. It was Stepney's long, speculative punt that would find its way to George Best to restore United's lead in extra time and break the resistance of an exhausted Benfica defence.

A year after Celtic had become the first British club to win the European Cup, Manchester United would be the first English club to win it.

MATT BUSBY'S EFFORTS TO REBUILD THE MANCHESTER UNITED TEAM WERE HELPED BY THE DISCOVERY OF GEORGE BEST, THE YOUNG GENIUS WHO HAD BEEN REJECTED BY GLENTORAN.

GLENTORAN FC

TRIALS TODAY

You may have dribbled around the entire defence and scored 16 goals with your charisma alone, but we just think you're a bit willowy...

BENFICA WERE WELL AWARE OF BEST'S ABILITY. HE HAD SHONE IN A 5-1 THRASHING OF THE EAGLES AT THE STADIUM OF LIGHT TWO YEARS EARLIER, DESTROYING THEIR DEFENCE WITH A DAZZLING DISPLAY FOR THE AGES.

TWINKLE

SWOON

Oh God.

UNITED HAD TO MAKE DO WITHOUT DENIS LAW, WHO WAS FORCED TO WATCH THE GAME ON TELEVISION FROM A HOSPITAL BED.

In many ways this is more fun than playing in the biggest match of my career. Also, please can I have some more morphine?

UNDETERRED, THEY TOOK THE LEAD THROUGH BOBBY CHARLTON, WHO USED HIS HEAD TO GREAT EFFECT.

JAIME GRAÇA STUNNED WEMBLEY WITH A 79TH MINUTE EQUALISER BUT THREE GOALS IN THE FIRST EIGHT MINUTES OF EXTRA-TIME CLINCHED VICTORY FOR UNITED. FIRST, BEST DRIBBLED AROUND THE BENFICA GOALKEEPER AND ROLLED THE BALL IN, LATER ADMITTING THAT HE CONSIDERED SCORING IN A MORE ELABORATE MANNER.

NUDGE

THEN, BRIAN KIDD - CELEBRATING HIS 19TH BIRTHDAY - NODDED IN UNITED'S THIRD. THIS YOUNG SUPERSTAR, DUBBED BY SOME AS 'THE FIFTH SHADOW', SOON AMASSED AN IMPRESSIVE CATALOGUE OF ANECDOTES ABOUT THE EXCESSES OF FAME AND FORTUNE...

Hm, tartan or paisley pyjamas tonight? Ah, my milky drink, thank you.

Oh, Mr Kidd. Where did it all go wrong?

IT WAS FITTING THAT HE SHOULD THEN SET UP BOBBY CHARLTON TO COMPLETE THE SCORING AND ROUND OFF A MOMENTOUS STORY OF RECOVERY.

THE WIN EARNED UNITED A PERMANENT PLACE IN THE HEART OF EVERY FOOTBALL FAN, ENSURING THAT NO ONE FOUND IT FUNNY WHEN THEY LATER LOST IN EUROPE TO VIDEOTON OR WOLFSBURG OR BASEL, OH NO.

WHAT A CARRY ON
ENGLAND 1970

England left nothing to chance in their quest to defend their world title, they'd struck a deal with Findus to provide all of their food and even shipped over their own team bus.

Upon landing in Mexico, immigration officials refused to believe Nobby Stiles was a footballer and Ramsey immediately set about winning hearts and minds. A local journalist welcomed him with a cheery 'Welcome to Mexico!' Ramsey shot back: 'You must be joking.' Cue a month of Mexican fans camping outside the England hotel, blasting their car horns.

This seemed to set the tone for the next few weeks, as England's plans slowly began to unravel. The food they'd sent over hadn't been cleared by local officials. The fishfingers and some ready meals were spared but the rest of it was burnt at the port, polluting the famously pure Mexican air with an acrid waft of incinerated Crispy Pancakes. Worse was to follow when Bobby Moore was arrested in Bogota under suspicion of stealing a bracelet from a jewellery shop. The very notion that an old-school Eastender would undertake such a caper was clearly ridiculous (without a shooter? For a bit of cheap tom? You mug). After a short time in custody he was released.

Most significant, though, was the stomach bug that struck down Gordon Banks on the eve of their quarter-final with West Germany. What caused his sickness remains a mystery. How could someone who had spent a month working in extreme heat, living purely off a diet of fishfingers and staying in a hotel staffed by insulted locals possibly fall ill?

After taking a two-goal lead, England seemed to be in control. Some English journalists even shouted *auf wiedersehen* at German supporters, because *they never learn*. However, England wilted in the heat of Léon and lost 3–2, Banks's replacement Peter Bonetti becoming the scapegoat for their elimination.

England's title defence had failed and they flew home to ruminate on a campaign that had been farcical enough to have been made into a film.

SHEER DELIGHTFUL FOOTBALL
BRAZIL 1970

Mexico '70 was the first World Cup to receive mass media coverage and the first to be broadcast in colour. Brazil were the epitome of this bright new era, with their thrilling football, shimmering yellow shirts and grey socks.

Mário Zagallo, who had won the World Cup as a player in 1958, was drafted in as a late replacement for coach João Saldanha, who had overseen the qualifying campaign. Saldanha was an explosive character who once threatened a player with a revolver, while manager of Botafogo. Upon learning of his dismissal from the Brazil job, he marched into the lobby of a Rio hotel with a loaded pistol, looking for his most vocal critics.

As ever, Brazil's preparations were meticulous. They spent a fortnight before the tournament sleeping and eating to their Mexican schedule (fishfingers?), their kit was redesigned to help them cope with Mexico's climate, and hand-made boots were crafted from special casts. Pelé, who had been convinced to return to the national fold, had an exclusive boot deal with Puma, leading some to grow suspicious at the regularity with which he bent down to tie his laces when the cameras were on him.

It was Pelé, along with Gérson and Carlos Alberto, who formed a committee of senior players who lobbied Zagallo with a suggested line-up. They called this group the Cobras because they were really, really tough and scary.

Brazil's approach of picking all their best players and letting them get on with it was a roaring success, though. They captivated the world with their attacking flair and set a standard rarely matched by the generations that followed. This is yet to be noticed by most of the broadcast media, who would have you believe that the *Seleção* still play as if Jairzinho was leading the line.

The Cobras. Jesus.

THE MILITARY REGIME OF BRAZIL WAS REFLECTED IN MÁRIO ZAGALLO'S BACKROOM STAFF FOR THE 1970 WORLD CUP. CAPTAIN CLÁUDIO COUTINHO AND ADMIRAL JERÔNIMO BASTOS WERE BOTH GIVEN ROLES.

THE SQUAD ALSO UNDERWENT A NASA TRAINING PROGRAMME, WHICH ADDED TO THEIR OTHER-WORLDLY LUSTRE.

Oh this hardly seems fair...

Altitude innit.

THEIR THRILLING RUN TO VICTORY WAS EPITOMISED BY THREE MOMENTS, BURNT INTO THE CONSCIOUSNESS OF ALL FOOTBALL SUPPORTERS:

1. PELÉ'S SHOT FROM THE HALF-WAY LINE AGAINST CZECHOSLOVAKIA.

2. PELÉ —AGAIN— DUMMYING URUGUAY'S GOALKEEPER, MAZURKIEWICZ IN THEIR SEMI-FINAL SUCCESS.

3. THEIR FOURTH GOAL IN THE FINAL AGAINST ITALY; A WHIRLWIND OF PASSING, MOVEMENT AND INDIVIDUAL BRILLIANCE, FINISHED WITH AN UNSTOPPABLE SHOT FROM CAPTAIN CARLOS ALBERTO. IT REMAINS THE BEST GOAL A WORLD CUP FINAL HAS WITNESSED.

The Cobras strike again!

You know that a nickname doesn't really count if you've given it to yourself, right?

COBRAS!

JAIRZINHO PELÉ CARLOS ALBERTO

RIVELINO

GERSON PELÉ

TOSTÃO CLODOALDO AGAIN (GOING ON A MAZY RUN PAST FOUR ITALIAN PLAYERS)

CLODOALDO

BRITO

BY WINNING THE WORLD CUP FOR THE THIRD TIME BRAZIL WERE PERMITTED TO KEEP THE JULES RIMET TROPHY PERMANENTLY.*

Where is the cup?

Mário, it's being looked after by top men.

Who?

Top. Men.

TOP MEN — QUALITY SHOES LOW PRICES

YES, WE CUT KEYS!

SO STYLE!

SEE OUR NEW BROGUES

ALSO; THE WORLD CUP

OPEN

* UNTIL IT WAS STOLEN AND MELTED DOWN IN 1983.

THE BIRTH OF
TOTAL FOOTBALL
AJAX 1970-1973

Under the guidance of British coach Vic Buckingham in the late fifties and early sixties, Ajax earned a reputation for playing open, attacking football and the development of talented local players. Whilst their football was attractive, it produced little silverware. This changed with the arrival of Rinus Michels.

The Dutchman was a disciplinarian but also created an environment of open discussion and critique (e.g. 'Johan, I'm feeling that you could have tracked back when their winger attacked the space.' 'Wim, I hear your frustration but I feel that you could have cut out the pass if you were able to turn more quickly than a grounded canal barge'). Most of his squad had come through Ajax's academy system and had a natural understanding of one another and the spaces they would occupy. It also helped that one of these players was Johan bloody Cruyff.

Cruyff had trained with Ajax from the age of ten and made his debut at seventeen. By the time he'd reached his early twenties he had mastered the game, so was able to elevate his thinking to ideas of systems and tactics. He was a god among men and, much like a god, he was really good at pointing.

AMSTERDAM EXPERIENCED SIGNIFICANT SOCIAL CHANGE IN THE 1960S, BREAKING FREE FROM THE SHACKLES OF POST-WAR CONSERVATISM TO BECOME A YOUTHFUL, TOLERANT CITY RENOWNED FOR PROGRESSIVE IDEAS.

AMSTERDAM CITY GOVERNMENT

Our street cleaners are severely underemployed. We need to attract more stag dos from the UK!

Yes! And students! Students who pass out after smelling one joss stick!

THIS NEW CLIMATE OF EXPERIMENT-ATION AND LONG HAIR WAS EPITOMISED BY THE AJAX TEAM OF THE EARLY 70S.

RINUS MICHELS HAD BEEN APPOINTED AS MANAGER IN 1965 AND INSTILLED A CULTURE OF PROFESSIONALISM. HE ALSO DEVELOPED A STYLE OF PLAY THAT WOULD SEE THEM CONQUER EUROPE. 'TOTAL FOOTBALL' WAS A SYSTEM IN WHICH PLAYERS WERE CONDIT-IONED TO BE COMFORTABLE PLAYING IN ANY POSITION.

DEFENCE

ATTACK

BOHEMIAN COFFEE SHOP

INTERPRETIVE DANCE PERFORMANCE

AJAX'S LEADER ON THE PITCH WAS JOHAN CRUYFF: A GIFTED, ANTI-AUTHORITY FIGURE WHO WOULD SPEND 90 MINUTES TALKING AND DIRECTING PLAY. ALTHOUGH A GENIUS, HE PROBABLY WASN'T THE EASIEST KIND OF PERSON TO WORK WITH.

Johan, did you eat my yogurt again?

I'll not be constrained by your patriarchal rule system, Janet.

THEIR DOMINANCE AT A DOMESTIC LEVEL WAS SOON TRANSLATED INTO CONTINENTAL SUCCESS. THEY WON THE FIRST OF THREE CONSECUTIVE EUROPEAN CUPS IN 1971 WITH A 2-0 WIN AT WEMBLEY AGAINST FERENC PUSKÁS'S PANATHINAIKOS.

MICHELS LEFT FOR BARCELONA AND WAS REPLACED BY ȘTEFAN KOVÁCS. THE NEW COACH SOON REALISED THAT THE PLAYERS KNEW WHAT THEY WERE DOING, SO ADOPTED MORE OF A 'HANDS OFF' APPROACH THAN HIS PREDECESSOR.

Academics posit that our style of play is intrinsically linked to Dutch attitudes to the use of space, as evidenced by architectural solutions...

I'd go furthe

Yeah. You lads carry on there.

AJAX WENT ON TO WIN THE EUROPEAN CUP IN 1972 AND 1973, BEATING INTER AND JUVENTUS RESPECTIVELY, BUT AFTER KOVÁCS' SUB-SEQUENT DEPARTURE, DIVISIONS BEGAN TO APPEAR IN THE DRESSING ROOM AND THEIR SUCCESS SOON WANED.

Who ate my yogurt?

BOB STOKOE'S RED LEGGINGS
SUNDERLAND 1 LEEDS 0, 1973

Leeds United weren't always a club trapped in a bleak cycle of self-loathing, megalomaniac owners and journeyman managers. For a spell in the early seventies Don Revie's side were one of the leading teams in the country, if not Europe. It came as a massive shock, then, when they lost the 1973 FA Cup final to second-tier Sunderland.

Surprisingly for a team that forged their success on a physical style and were not averse to feigning injuries or intimidating officials, Leeds were not universally loved. Revie dismissed this criticism as a form of tall poppy syndrome, but this particular tall poppy wasn't above sneakily yanking his opponent's armpit hairs.

Sunderland's manager Bob Stokoe also had a personal beef with Revie. He frequently alleged that, while managing Bury in 1962, Revie had approached him with an offer of £500 to 'go easy' before a match against Leeds. Stokoe claimed he refused and became enraged when Revie asked to speak to the Bury players directly. The accusations were, of course, denied but it did add some extra spice to the contest.

Sunderland's run to Wembley was no fluke; they'd overcome leading clubs Manchester City and Arsenal in earlier rounds. The evening before the final, during a televised preview, Jack Charlton and Brian Clough had predicted an easy win for Leeds. The eyes of the watching Sunderland players narrowed, their flares flared; this would be no walkover. Nervous excitement overtook some of the players. Defender Micky Horswill later recalled staying up all night with team-mate Joe Bolton, eating sweets and watching television. This was 1973, though, so they must have been watching the test card after about 11pm.

DON REVIE BECAME LEEDS MANAGER IN 1961, AGED JUST 33. BY THE TIME OF THE 1973 FA CUP FINAL, HE HAD TRANSFORMED THEM INTO ONE OF ENGLAND'S BEST TEAMS. AS AN INNOVATOR, HE HAD INTRODUCED MANY GROUNDBREAKING IDEAS, SUCH AS:

• GIVING PLAYERS DOSSIERS ON OPPONENTS,

• TEAM BONDING ACTIVITIES, INCLUDING CARPET BOWLS

• WIN-AT-ALL-COSTS CYNICISM

• KIT DESIGN

BUT SUNDERLAND'S MANAGER, BOB STOKOE, ALSO KNEW A THING OR TWO ABOUT FASHION. HE TURNED OUT AT WEMBLEY IN AN OUTFIT THAT IN NO WAY LOOKED LIKE HE HAD AWOKEN NAKED IN A CHARITY SHOP DONATION BIN.

CONCEALED COMB-OVER

TRILBY

LEEDS TOP ??

TIGHT RED TRACKSUIT

COLUMBO-STYLE TRENCH COAT

GREY BLANKET

TAPERED LEG

BLACK SHOES

Even by the standards of 1973, that is spectacular.

SUNDERLAND PRODUCED ONE OF THE BIGGEST SHOCKS IN FA CUP HISTORY WITH A 1-0 WIN. THE VITAL GOAL CAME AFTER 31 MINUTES, IAN PORTERFIELD DRILLING IN A SHOT FROM 8 YARDS. HE LATER ADMITTED ON TV THAT IT WAS THE FIRST TIME HE'D EVER FELT REAL EMOTION.

More tea, Mrs Porterfield?

ON AIR

Shove it.

LEEDS BOMBARDED THE SUNDERLAND GOAL WITH SHOTS BUT WERE DENIED BY GOALKEEPER JIM MONTGOMERY; A MIRACULOUS DOUBLE SAVE MIDWAY THROUGH THE SECOND HALF SIGNALLED THAT IT WAS NOT TO BE LEEDS' DAY.

UPON THE FINAL WHISTLE, STOKOE SKIPPED ACROSS THE PITCH, TRENCH COAT FLAPPING BEHIND HIM, TO EMBRACE MONT-GOMERY. THE TEAM CELEBRATED WITH A BURGER ON OXFORD STREET AT 2AM AND AN AWAY GAME AT CARDIFF TWO DAYS LATER.

I asked for no gherkin!

I think I preferred it when he was a dispassionate husk.

LEEDS RECOVERED AND WON THE LEAGUE TITLE THE FOLLOWING SEASON, PERHAPS HELPED BY DON REVIE'S INTRODUCTION OF SOCK TAGS TO THE KIT.

This. Changes. Everything.

TOTAL FUCKWITS
WEST GERMANY 2 NETHERLANDS 1, 1974

One-nil up against West Germany and in complete control, the Netherlands opted to mess about rather than win the World Cup their football deserved. Johnny Rep later admitted: 'We wanted to make fun of the Germans. We didn't consciously think about it but we did it. We kept passing the ball around and passing the ball around. We forgot to score the second goal.'

West Germany weren't exactly stooges though. They were the reigning European champions and their team included six players who had won the European Cup with Bayern Munich just a few weeks earlier. This wasn't Port Vale the Dutch were toying with.

The Netherlands' over-confidence may have been based on the fact that their route to the final had been a relative stroll, conceding just a solitary goal on the way (an own goal against Bulgaria by Ruud Krol, who presumably did it to make things more interesting). West Germany had made harder work of it, suffering from a poor start and player indiscipline.

The fact that West Germany recovered to win the final seems to have become a historical footnote, though. This game and this tournament was all about the Netherlands. Recalling the game forty years later, Johan Cruyff pondered: 'Maybe we were the real winners in the end. I think the world remembers our team more.'

HOLLAND'S TEAM OF 1974 WAS ONE OF THE GREATEST SIDES TO NOT WIN THE WORLD CUP. AND LIKE THE EXALTED HUNGARY TEAM OF THE 1950s, THEY WERE DENIED BY...

The Germans!

DASTARDLY SPOILSPORTS

EUROPEAN CHAMPIONS

AS GOOD AS HOLLAND

Boo! HISS!

RINUS MICHELS' NETHERLANDS CRUISED TO THE FINAL; THEIR 'TOTAL FOOTBALL' DELIGHTING THE WORLD. THEIR CONFIDENCE WAS ILLUSTRATED BY CRUYFF'S FAMOUS TURN THAT SO BAFFLED SWEDEN'S OLSSON.

WEST GERMANY'S ROUTE WAS LESS SMOOTH. THE PLAYERS WERE IN REVOLT OVER BONUS PAYMENTS AND AFTER A HUMILIATING 1-0 DEFEAT TO EAST GERMANY IN THE GROUP STAGE, MANAGER HELMUT SCHÖN REFUSED TO LEAVE HIS HOTEL ROOM.

Come on, Helmut, we're sorry.

Go away.

DO NOT DISTURB

WATER-SHIP DOWN

STILL, THEY RECOVERED TO MAKE IT THROUGH TO THE FINAL, WHERE FEW OBSERVERS GAVE THEM MUCH OF A CHANCE.

ON THE EVE OF THE GAME, THE DUTCH CAMP WAS FORCED TO DENY GERMAN TABLOID ALLEGATIONS THAT FOUR PLAYERS HAD TAKEN PART IN A 'NAKED POOL PARTY' WITH FOUR GERMAN WOMEN.

Johan. Your wife's on the phone. Something about a newspaper report...

HOWEVER, THEY TOOK THE LEAD BEFORE WEST GERMANY HAD EVEN TOUCHED THE BALL. ULI HOENESS TRIPPED CRUYFF AND REFEREE JACK TAYLOR AWARDED A PENALTY. BECKENBAUER WAS UNIMPRESSED EVIDENTLY...

You are an Englishman.

DESPITE THEIR DOMINATION, HOLLAND FAILED TO ADD A SECOND GOAL AND WEST GERMANY WERE AWARDED A PENALTY OF THEIR OWN AFTER 25 MINUTES, WHICH BREITNER TUCKED AWAY.

We Germans have always respected your culture, cuisine and beer.

THE GREAT GERD MÜLLER THEN ROLLED A SHOT IN TO PUT THE HOSTS AHEAD, HOLLAND COULDN'T FIND A WAY BACK AND THE GERMANS WERE CROWNED CHAMPIONS. LATER, A ROW BROKE OUT WHEN THE DFB BARRED THE GERMAN PLAYERS' WIVES FROM THE POST-MATCH BANQUET.

The players have all stormed off to a bar. What should we do now?

Naked pool party?

BAVARIAN BRILLIANCE
BAYERN MUNICH 1974-1976

The Bayern Munich team that won a hat-trick of European Cups in the mid-seventies rarely receives the plaudits of the other great sides that preceded them.

If there was a perception that their wins in the finals were lucky, to reach that stage on three consecutive occasions was a remarkable achievement. Take, for example, the first of their victories in 1974: before facing Atlético Madrid in the decider, they had to overcome Åtvidaberg (on penalties), Dynamo Dresden, CSKA Sofia and Újpesti Dózsa. No pushovers there.

Leeds United supporters still seethe about the events of the 1975 final. They must have a case because if there's one thing you don't expect from Yorkshiremen, it's a longstanding sense of resentment.

There was even some bitterness about the win that completed Bayern's trio of European crowns the following year. Their opponents, Saint-Étienne, blamed the design of the Hampden Park goals for their defeat. They maintained that if the posts had rounded edges, rather than squared ones, a Jacques Santini header that hit the upright when the game was goalless would have gone in.

By this stage it appears that even the Bayern fans had grown jaded with success, as the welcome they received upon their return to Munich was flatter than a tuba note on the last day of Oktoberfest. In fairness, think how bored you'd feel if *your* club won three European Cups in a row.

WHEN BAYERN MUNICH LOST 4-0 TO AJAX AT THE QUARTER-FINAL STAGE OF THE 1973 EUROPEAN CUP, THEIR GOALKEEPER - SEPP MAIER-WAS SO FURIOUS THAT HE TOSSED HIS KIT AND BOOTS INTO A SMALL POND OUTSIDE THE TEAM HOTEL.

PERHAPS IT WAS THIS BIG DRAMATIC GESTURE THAT HELPED TO INSPIRE BAYERN TO WIN THE NEXT THREE EUROPEAN CUPS.

Nothing demands respect like a grown adult throwing a tantrum in public. We'd better raise our game.

THE BAYERN TEAM MOSTLY COMPRISED PLAYERS FROM THE LOCAL REGION AND INCLUDED THE SPINE OF THE SUCCESSFUL WEST GERMAN TEAM. AS WELL AS MAIER, THERE WAS:

FRANZ BECKENBAUER — 'DER KAISER'

GERD MÜLLER — 'DER BOMBER'

PAUL BREITNER — 'DER AFRO'

ULI HOENESS — 'DER CREATIVE ACCOUNTAN[T]'

BAYERN'S RUN WAS NEARLY SNUFFED OUT IN THEIR FIRST FINAL. A STUNNING LAST-GASP EQUALISER FROM DEFENDER SCHWARZENBECK (AKA 'THE KAISER'S CLEANER') SAVED THEM AGAINST ATLÉTICO MADRID.

Nice goal. I hate to mention it, but there's still a tide mark on my bath tub, so...

You know it's just a nickname, right?

Yep.

THEY WON THE REPLAY 4-0 AND BECAME THE FIRST BUNDES-LIGA CLUB TO LIFT THE EUROPEAN CUP.

THE TEAM REMAINED LARGELY UNCHANGED, BUT THE PIPE-SMOKING MAOIST, PAUL BREITNER, DID LEAVE FOR REAL MADRID.

If there's one club that symbolises the rejection of personal wealth for collective social need, it's Real Madrid.

BAYERN PREVAILED IN A CONTROVERSIAL 2-0 WIN AGAINST LEEDS, WHO HAD TWO PENALTY CLAIMS TURNED DOWN AND A GOAL DISALLOWED. THEIR FANS TOOK IT QUITE WELL, THOUGH.

THERE WAS A SUBDUED MOOD AMONG THE BAYERN PLAYERS AFTER THEIR 1-0 WIN AGAINST ST. ÉTIENNE. THEY SENSED THEIR STORY HAD RUN ITS COURSE. THE CLUB PRESIDENT EVEN WARNED THEM OF THE PERILS OF 'WINNING TOO MUCH'.

It's unhealthy to be always happy. It's why you don't see many Australian poets.

Right, yeah. Hey, is there a pond round here?

HOT CHIP
THE PANENKA

As everyone knows, penalty shoot-outs are a lottery. The confidence needed to perform a basic element of your job cannot be instilled through repeated practice. Players might as well close their eyes and take a hopeful swing at the ball, such is the randomness of the penalty shoot-out.

One player who bucked this trend was Czechoslovakia's Antonín Panenka. His innovation of chipping the ball over a goalkeeper's dive proved to be a failsafe way of winning that lottery, just like buying a hundred tickets.

This technique has now become commonplace. Great 'Panenka' kicks we have known include:

- Zinedine Zidane's effort that hit the crossbar and just dropped over the line in the 2006 World Cup final.
- Andrea Pirlo dinking one over a prancing Joe Hart at the 2012 European Championship.
- Gary Lineker completely blowing his chance to equal the England goal-scoring record by floating a soft shot directly into the arms of a baffled Taffarel during a friendly with Brazil in 1992.

Panenka's chip was first used in the 1976 European Championship final in a shoot-out against West Germany. Sepp Maier's humiliation, and Uli Hoeness's miss, instilled a resolve in the German national team to never again lose in this manner. Since then they have emerged victorious from shoot-outs against France (1982), Mexico (1986), England (1990 and 1996), Argentina (2006) and Italy (2016). German goalkeeping coach Andreas Köpke attributes their excellent record to *nervenstaerke* (strength of nerves) and self-confidence, but some people are just really good at doing the lottery.

AFTER MORE THAN 100 YEARS OF ORGANISED FOOTBALL, PEOPLE PROBABLY THOUGHT THAT THERE WAS NO TRICK, FLICK, SKILL OR MOVE LEFT UNTRIED.

WHOA!

NO! NO!
Yep.

Well that's just dangerous.

BUT IN 1976, CZECHOSLOVAKIA'S ANTONÍN PANENKA UNVEILED AN INGENIOUS METHOD OF PENALTY-TAKING THAT WOULD SEE HIM BECOME PART OF THE GAME'S VERY LANGUAGE.

PANENKA PRACTISED PENALTIES EACH DAY AFTER TRAINING. HE USED TO BET ON THE OUTCOME WITH THE GOALKEEPER, WITH THE STAKE BEING BEER AND CHOCOLATE. TIRED OF LOSING, THE MIDFIELDER DEVELOPED HIS NEW TECHNIQUE.

DINK

BEER
CHOC

HE HONED THE ROUTINE AT CLUB LEVEL, BUT IT WASN'T UNTIL THE EUROPEAN CHAMPIONSHIP FINAL THAT HE WOULD REVEAL IT TO THE WIDER WORLD.

CZECHOSLOVAKIA AND WEST GERMANY HAD PLAYED OUT A HARD-FOUGHT 2-2 DRAW. AS EXTRA-TIME ENDED, THE CZECH PLAYERS LEFT THE FIELD, UNAWARE THAT THE TWO ASSOCIATIONS HAD AGREED TO SETTLE THE MATCH WITH PENALTIES.

OK, capricciosa or meat feast?
Um, lads...
PIZZA

ALL THE PENALTIES WERE CONVERTED UNTIL ULI HOENESS SKIED THE GERMANS' FOURTH. FRANZ BECKENBAUER, MAKING HIS HUNDREDTH INTERNATIONAL APPEARANCE, HAD BEEN DOWN TO TAKE THE KICK ORIGINALLY.

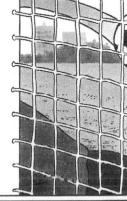

It's OK, Uli; my humility is legendary. We all make mistakes.
Really?
Well; not me, obviously.

UP STEPPED PANENKA. AS SEPP MAIER DIVED TO HIS LEFT, PANENKA CHIPPED THE BALL INTO THE NET. CZECHOSLOVAKIA WERE EUROPEAN CHAMPIONS.

YEARS LATER, PANENKA NOTED THAT HAD HE MISSED, THE CZECH COMMUNIST PARTY MAY HAVE FORCED HIM TO QUIT THE GAME AND WORK IN A FACTORY.

Right Panenka, I want 500 sturdy socialist two-by-fours by the end of your shift.

Delicate chip

THE RED MACHINE
LIVERPOOL IN EUROPE 1977-1984

The history of Liverpool Football Club is linked intrinsically with glory on the European stage. Memories of those electric nights at Anfield permeate; the roar of The Kop being equal to a goal advantage, a fact often criminally overlooked when aggregate scores are tallied.

The sickly-sweet home-made banners of the Reds faithful have undone many a visiting continental team, as if their saccharine slogans had been hand-written on flypaper. It's no coincidence that when Liverpool FC are leading the march in Europe, the driveways of Merseyside bedsheet salesmen are adorned with new cars.

Liverpool won the European Cup four times between 1977 and 1984. They also won the UEFA Cup in 1973 and 1976. Their supremacy made them one of the most feared clubs in the world and their style of play garnered widespread respect. (Paul Breitner: 'English football is stupid!') After vanquishing Real Madrid in the 1981 final, one French commentator described the match as 'chloroform football', presumably because the quality of entertainment was as dizzying as watching an entire boxset of Carla Lane sitcoms in one sitting. They really were that good.

WHEN BILL SHANKLY ANNOUNCED HIS SHOCK RESIGNATION AS LIVERPOOL MANAGER IN 1974, SEVERAL PEOPLE WERE CONSIDERED FOR THE ROLE, INCLUDING JACK CHARLTON.

THE BOOT ROOM

it long into the 'channels

INSTEAD, THEY HIRED BOB PAISLEY, WHO WOULD BECOME THE MOST SUCCESSFUL MANAGER IN THE CLUB'S HISTORY.

HE WON THE FIRST OF THREE EUROPEAN CUPS IN 1977, OVERCOMING THE NEWS THAT STAR PLAYER KEVIN KEEGAN INTENDED TO MOVE ABROAD AT THE END OF THE SEASON, CITING THE UK TAX RATE FOR HIGH EARNERS AS A REASON.

I will love it if someone else pays for schools and hospitals; love it.

AT THE QUARTER-FINAL STAGE, LIVERPOOL WERE TRAILING ST ÉTIENNE ON AWAY GOALS. FACING ELIMINATION, PAISLEY SENT ON DAVID FAIRCLOUGH, WHO BAGGED THE GOAL TO SEND THEM THROUGH. FAIRCLOUGH'S KNACK FOR SCORING FROM OFF THE BENCH EARNED HIM THE NICKNAME 'SUPERSUB', WHICH HE GREW TO LOATHE.

Right, David, the squad's been hit by a flu epidemic. We only have 11 fit men, so your role will be crucial.

You'll start on the bench. Being a man light, the lads will tire in the second half and that's when you'll come on!

SUPER SUB!

THE REDS THEN SWEPT ASIDE FC ZURICH TO SET UP A FINAL WITH BORUSSIA MÖNCHENGLADBACH IN ROME. BEFORE THE GAME PAISLEY QUIPPED THAT THE LAST TIME HE'D BEEN IN THE CITY HE WAS IN A TANK, NOT SPECIFYING WHETHER THIS WAS DURING THE WAR.

ROME OLYMPICS 1960

KEEGAN WAS HUGELY INFLUENTIAL IN HIS LAST GAME FOR THE CLUB, PULLING APART GLADBACH'S DEFENCE AND TORMENTING HIS MARKER, BERTI VOGTS.

I mean, it's not that I'm against tax per se, it's just that it seems to punish people who work hard and do well for themselves.

LIVERPOOL WON 3-1, REWARDING THEIR 30,000 FANS WHO HAD MADE THE TRIP, IN SCENES REMINISCENT OF THE EXODUS OF CELTIC FANS IN 1967.

Cardinal, why is there a hot air balloon in my square?

It's a mystery, Your Holiness.

What is this, a frikkin Dan Brown novel?

'Dan'...?

THE JUNTA'S WORLD CUP
ARGENTINA 1978

In 1976 a military dictatorship took control of Argentina. Thousands of people were tortured, murdered and disappeared as part of the junta's 'Dirty War' against dissenters. FIFA – never an organisation to put ethics before profit – decided that this nation, soaked in the blood of human suffering, was the ideal location for the world's biggest sports competition.

Amnesty International sent evidence of the injustices to journalists departing for the tournament. While the report was unsettling for some, others chose to endorse the regime, including – knock me down with a propaganda leaflet – Henry Kissinger and the Pope. The Catholic Church in Argentina compared the coup to the resurrection of Christ.

Despite suggestions that some players and teams would boycott the World Cup on humanitarian grounds, none did. These were very different times, though; modern footballers have more of a moral conscience – good luck getting any of them to play in a World Cup hosted by an oppressive, unelected government now!

FIFA AWARDED THE HOSTING RIGHTS FOR THE 1978 WORLD CUP TO ARGENTINA BEFORE A MILITARY COUP SEIZED POWER OF THE COUNTRY. BUT AS SOON AS NEWS EMERGED OF HUMAN RIGHTS ABUSES, FIFA TOOK SWIFT AND DECISIVE ACTION.

THE ARGENTINIAN JUNTA'S REGIME OF TORTURE AND MURDER

THE PRESIDENT OF THE ORGANISING COMMITTEE, CAPTAIN CARLOS LACOSTE, SPENT $700 MILLION ON THE TOURNAMENT. THE ORIGINAL BUDGET WAS $70-100 MILLION. HE WAS LATER FOUND GUILTY OF DIVERTING FUNDS TO THE JUNTA AND POCKETING $4 MILLION FOR HIMSELF.

I'll have that.

HAVE A WILD GUESS WHO SPOKE IN HIS DEFENCE AT THE TRIAL.

YEP, FIFA PRESIDENT JOÃO HAVELANGE.

Seriously, I make Sepp Blatter look like Erin Brockovich.

THE REGIME'S LEADER, GENERAL VIDELA, HIRED AN AMERICAN FIRM TO PUBLICISE THE TOURNAMENT, WHICH HAD BECOME A PR EXERCISE FOR THE JUNTA.

XI Campeonato Mundial de Fútbol Junio 1978

Argentina '78

IN ROSARIO, SLUM DWELLINGS WERE HIDDEN BEHIND A WALL PAINTED WITH SMILING FACES. THE INHABITANTS WERE SHIPPED OUT TO CITIES THAT WEREN'T HOSTING WORLD CUP MATCHES OR WERE DISAPPEARED COMPLETELY.

See; it's fiiiiiine.

DETAINEES IN THE TORTURE CENTRE AT THE ARGENTINIAN NAVY MECHANICAL SCHOOL IN BUENOS AIRES COULD HEAR THE ROAR OF THE HOME CROWD AND WOULD JOIN IN CHANTS FROM THEIR CELLS AS AN ACT OF DEFIANCE.

Ar-gen-tina, Ar-gen-tina...!

GENERAL VIDELA DIED IN PRISON IN 2013, BUT LACOSTE RETAINED HIS LINKS WITH ARGENTINIAN SOCCER AND WAS EVEN THEIR REPRESENTATIVE AT THE DRAW FOR THE 1986 WORLD CUP. HE DIED A FREE MAN IN 2004.

Carlos, old friend. They let you keep the hat; wonderful.

FIFA

AS FOR FIFA, THEY LEARNED THEIR LESSON AND NEVER AGAIN GAVE HOSTING RIGHTS TO A NATION GUILTY OF HUMAN RIGHTS VIOLATIONS.

2022 FIFA WORLD CUP

QATAR

ALLY'S TARTAN ARMY
SCOTLAND FAIL TO WIN 1978 WORLD CUP

Despite the overwhelming home advantage enjoyed by Argentina, it was Scotland who were definitely going to win the 1978 World Cup. Their effusive manager, Ally MacLeod, had whipped the nation up into an uncharacteristic state of optimism. His management style was based on motivational speeches and confident one-liners ('My name is Ally MacLeod and I'm a winner'), rather than tactical instruction. It provides us with a window into what life will be like when Tim Sherwood becomes an international manager.

Scotland's positive outlook was to some extent justified. The squad contained bona fide world-class players in Kenny Dalglish and a young Graeme Souness, and MacLeod was confident of overcoming their first two group phase opponents of Peru ('old men') and Iran ('minnows'). By the time they faced the Netherlands in their third match, the group would surely be sewn up.

Off they set, to tremendous fanfare, the squad only mildly distracted by all the advertising work they had done for carpets and cameras and cars and beer and fags. This was their year. What could possibly go wrong?

SCOTLAND WENT TO THE 1978 WORLD CUP ON A WAVE OF OPTIMISM, GENERATED IN PART BY THE BOUNDLESS POSITIVITY AND COCKY SOUNDBITES OF MANAGER ALLY MACLEOD.

What will you do if you win the World Cup?

Retain it.

AS THE ONLY BRITISH NATION TO HAVE QUALIFIED, THE SCOTS WERE NO DOUBT THRILLED TO RECEIVE THE TEMPORARY SUPPORT OF PEOPLE SOUTH OF THE BORDER.

My great grandmother was from Clyde and I'm partial to a 'wee' bit of shortbread, so I've always felt an affinity with the Scotch.

THE TEAM WERE EVEN THE SUBJECT OF A HIT RECORD. COMEDIAN ANDY CAMERON'S 'ALLY'S TARTAN ARMY' REACHED NUMBER 6 IN THE CHARTS AND WAS PERFORMED TO A GROUP OF BEMUSED TEENAGE GIRLS ON 'TOP OF THE POPS'.

This is literally the worst thing that could happen today.

30,000 FANS WAVED THE SQUAD OFF AT HAMPDEN PARK, BUT WHEN THEY ARRIVED IN ARGENTINA THE TEAM BUS BROKE DOWN AND HAD TO BE PUSHED UP A HILL TO THEIR HOTEL.

It's a good job Ally says we're going to win the World Cup or this could be translated as some sort of gloomy omen.

MACLEOD HADN'T SCOUTED THEIR FIRST OPPONENTS, PERU. WITH THE SCORES LEVEL AT HALF-TIME, HIS ADVICE TO GOALKEEPER ALAN ROUGH WAS TO KICK THE BALL HARDER TO BYPASS PERU'S DOMINANT MIDFIELD, BUT ROUGH WAS POWERLESS TO STOP TWO SECOND-HALF ROCKETS FROM TEÓFILO CUBILLAS.

Alan! Alan! THAT'S how hard I want you to kick it!

SCOTLAND LOST 3-1. FORWARD WILLIE JOHNSTON WAS THEN SENT HOME FOR FAILING A DRUG TEST; THEY COULD ONLY DRAW 1-1 WITH IRAN; AND MACLEOD WAS BITTEN BY A DOG IN THE POST-MATCH INTERVIEW. THEY NOW NEEDED TO BEAT HOLLAND BY THREE GOALS IN ORDER TO PROGRESS.

FINALLY, EVERYTHING CLICKED AND THEY JUSTIFIED THEIR HYPE. AFTER 68 MINUTES, ARCHIE GEMMILL SKIPPED THROUGH THE DUTCH DEFENCE TO SCORE ONE OF THE ALL-TIME GREAT WORLD CUP GOALS AND PUT THE SCOTS 3-1 UP. THEY ONLY NEEDED ONE MORE GOAL!

I haven't felt this good since Joe Jordan won a highly dubious penalty against Wales to enable our qualification

ALAS, JOHNNY REP PULLED ONE BACK ALMOST IMMEDIATELY AND THAT WAS THAT. DISAPPOINTING THOUGH THE EXPERIENCE WAS, GIVEN SCOTLAND'S FORM IN RECENT YEARS, IT AT LEAST REPRESENTED A GLORIOUS FAILURE, RATHER THAN JUST FAILURE.

What will you do if you qualify for the World Cup?

Spontaneously combust.

GENERAL DELIGHT
ARGENTINA WIN THE 1978 WORLD CUP

A feel-good story for the ages: the team enjoying the patronage of a savage right-wing dictatorship is crowned world champions, despite all the odds being stacked in their favour. Let the tickertape fly.

Not that the Argentinian players had any choice in the matter. The regime had issued them with barely veiled threats; failure would have consequences. Defender Alberto Tarantini was acutely aware of the dangers, as some of his friends had been disappeared. Argentina's coach César Luis Menotti also faced pressure from the generals, but did his best to protect his players.

Politically, Menotti was completely at odds with the generals, but they tolerated him because he represented the best chance of an Argentinian victory. Menotti justified his involvement in this propaganda exercise as being a way to remind the people of the freedoms they had once enjoyed.

The players did commit some small, but significant, acts of defiance. At the final, they had been ordered to look towards the generals, reclining in the VIP section of the stand; instead they turned their attention to the terraces, where the people stood. Later, after giving the regime its prize, several players refused the handshake of General Videla. The Pope must have been furious.

THE COLD HAND OF THE MILITARY DICTATORSHIP LOOMED LARGE OVER ARGENTINA'S 1978 WORLD CUP WIN. ALLEGATIONS OF MATCH-FIXING, DOPING AND WIDESPREAD SHITEHOUSERY PERSIST TO THIS DAY.

FOR EXAMPLE, AFTER THEIR CONTROVERSIAL GROUP STAGE WIN AGAINST FRANCE, THE URINE TEST OF ONE ARGENTINIAN PLAYER APPARENTLY REVEALED THAT HE WAS PREGNANT.

Heh, well, yes; I suppose there is a first time for everything.

MOST OF THE ALLEGATIONS FOCUS ON THE MATCH WITH PERU, WHICH ARGENTINA HAD TO WIN BY FOUR GOALS IN ORDER TO REACH THE FINAL. GENERAL VIDELA VISITED THE PERU TEAM BEFORE THE GAME.

Guys! I just thought: some of you probably have families in Argentina. Just sayin'.

THE SUNDAY TIMES LATER CLAIMED THAT ON THE EVE OF THE MATCH THE JUNTA HAD SENT PERU A HUGE SHIPMENT OF GRAIN AND HAD UNFROZEN $50 MILLION OF CREDIT. ARGENTINA WON 6-0.

Hah! All they had to do was kick the ball over our midfield!

THE NETHERLANDS WERE ALL THAT STOOD BETWEEN THE GENERALS AND THE REFLECTED GLORY OF A WORLD CUP WIN. PRE-MATCH SHENANIGANS THEREFORE INCLUDED:

A SUCCESSFUL PROTEST THAT THE ISRAELI REF BE DROPPED, DUE TO ISRAEL'S CLOSE RELATIONSHIP WITH HOLLAND.

Football and politics shouldn't mix

THE DUTCH TEAM BUS TAKING THE SCENIC ROUTE TO THE VENUE.

DANIEL PASSARELLA SUBMITTING A FORMAL COMPLAINT ABOUT RENÉ VAN DER KERKHOF'S PLASTER CAST.

But I've worn it for the last five games!

It's dangerous. Some of our players are pregnant!

ARGENTINA LEAVING THE PITCH FOR FIVE MINUTES WHILE THE ISSUE WAS SORTED, WITH THE DUTCH TEAM STRANDED IN FRONT OF THE HOSTILE HOME CROWD.

BOOOOO

HOLLAND FOUGHT BRAVELY, THOUGH, AND NEARLY SNATCHED A VICTORY. WITH JUST SECONDS REMAINING AND THE SCORE TIED AT 1-1, ROB RENSENBRINK CRACKED A SHOT AGAINST THE POST.

General, the Dutch say they're 'all right for grain, thanks'.

BUT EXTRA-TIME GOALS FROM KEMPES AND BERTONI WON THE GAME FOR THE HOSTS AND THE GENERALS HAD THEIR MOMENT OF GLORY. THE WIN AT LEAST BROUGHT SOME JOY TO THE OPPRESSED ARGENTINIAN PEOPLE.

Yaaaay...!

SHOWBIZ SOCCER
THE NASL

The North American Soccer League of 1968–1984 offered glitz, glamour and team names as exotic as the New England Tea Men, San Diego Jaws and the Tulsa Roughnecks.

At the height of its popularity, it attracted a crowd of 77,000 people and the star-spangled New York Cosmos averaged attendances of over 40,000 for three straight seasons; a previously unimaginable feat. The Warner Brothers-backed Cosmos were somehow able to entice Pelé out of retirement with a compelling vision and a pile of cash as big as an American breakfast ($2.8 million for three years).

Other clubs tried to compete with the Cosmos, paying huge salaries to attract foreign stars. Pelé was joined in the NASL by, among others, Franz Beckenbauer, Johan Cruyff, George Best, Eusébio, Bobby Moore and Gerd Müller. In a purely footballing sense the most successful import was the controversial Italian striker, Giorgio Chinaglia. Odd that a person so enamoured with guns would thrive in the US.

NASL administrators felt they needed to sell the sport to the American public, so they introduced rule changes and gimmicks, such as clocks counting down to zero, a thirty-five-metre line for offsides, penalty shoot-outs to decide drawn matches and a points system whereby bonus points were awarded for scoring goals.

The league lasted until 1984, when the effects of over-expansion, over-spending (some clubs were spending as much as 70 per cent of their budget on salaries) and an economic recession took hold.

Although the NASL failed, it did increase the popularity of the sport in the US and provided lessons for the successful Major League Soccer, which would not be so reliant on ageing stars looking for one last payday.

A BUNCH OF REASONS WHY THE NASL WAS RAD

THIS BALL

THESE KITS

MORE INTERNATIONAL SUPERSTARS THAN YOU COULD SHAKE AN ENORMOUS SALARY PACKAGE AT.

PELÉ!

BEST!

BECKENBAUER!

KEITH WELLER!

EVIL GENIUS GIORGIO CHINAGLIA

HUGE CROWDS, INCLUDING CELEBRITIES!

REDFORD!

STREISAND!

ALI!

TRUMP!

You want to hear again how I could probably fly if I put my mind to it? Hey, what kind of a name is 'Muhammad' anyway?

THE FACT THAT JOHAN CRUYFF PLAYED FOR A TEAM CALLED 'THE DIPLOMATS'.

Darn it, Johan; did you eat my frogurt?

Go fuck yourself, Tommy.

THE OPPORTUNITIES FOR EUROPEAN SNOBBERY.

Top-flight football in England will never be reduced to a hyperbolic parade of overpaid foreign players. You can keep your polyester mascots, we're quite happy with our crumbling deathtrap stadiums, thank you.

NOTTINGHAM FOREST, CHAMPIONS OF EUROPE
YES, REALLY

At the time of writing, Nottingham Forest sit in seventeenth position in the Championship table. They are without a permanent manager; their fans bereft of hope. In order to replicate the success of the Brian Clough era, they would need to win the Premier League within three years and then win the Champions League twice in a row. While Leicester City have shown that it is possible for a provincial club from the East Midlands to shock the modern football elite, there is as much chance of this happening as there is of Andy Reid winning the *Ballon d'Or*.

The Forest team that won the 1979 European Cup was largely made up of journeymen and players who had previously underachieved. Frank Clark had been released by Newcastle, Larry Lloyd was a big-boned centre-back and striker Gary Birtles was a part-time carpet fitter signed from non-league Long Eaton for £2,000. They performed beyond all expectations alongside international players like Archie Gemmill, Viv Anderson, Martin O'Neill and Tony Woodcock. Clough was also given money to bring in the likes of Peter Shilton and Trevor Francis. Together, this band of unremarkable men would take Europe by storm. There's hope for Andy Reid yet.

BRIAN CLOUGH'S METHODS MAY HAVE BEEN UNORTHODOX...

CLOUGH WAS A SUPREME ORGANISER AND MOTIVATOR; HIS UNPREDICTABILITY BEING PART OF HIS LEGEND.

BUT HE REMAINS ONE OF THE FINEST MANAGERS BRITISH FOOTBALL HAS EVER SEEN.

UNDER THE GUIDANCE OF CLOUGH AND HIS ASSISTANT, PETER TAYLOR, NOTTINGHAM FOREST WENT FROM BEING SECOND DIVISION STRUGGLERS TO EUROPEAN CHAMPIONS IN JUST FOUR YEARS. THE PAIR WERE MASTERS AT TRANSFORMING ORDINARY PLAYERS INTO WORLD-BEATERS. FOR EXAMPLE, JOHN ROBERTSON WENT FROM THIS...

...TO THIS:

Hard work and diet custard, losers.

What's his secret?!

AFTER WINNING THE LEAGUE TITLE AT THE FIRST ATTEMPT, CLOUGH'S FOREST WENT ON TO LIFT THE EUROPEAN CUP IN 1979. HE WOULD TREAT EUROPEAN TIES LIKE MINI-HOLIDAYS, ENCOURAGING THE PLAYERS TO ENJOY THEMSELVES.

Big Frankie Clark on tour! What time's the foam party?

We're in Liverpool, Frank. 9 o'clock.

IN THE SEMI-FINAL THEY FELL 2-0 BEHIND TO COLOGNE WITHIN THE FIRST 20 MINUTES.

Fetch my axe.

BUT THEY FOUGHT BACK TO DRAW 3-3 AND THEN WON THE RETURN LEG 1-0.

FOREST OVER-CAME MALMÖ IN THE FINAL. TREVOR FRANCIS STOOPED TO HEAD IN THE ONLY GOAL, BARELY CARING ABOUT GRAZING HIMSELF ON THE HAMMER-THROWING RING BESIDE THE GOAL.

Drink this, lad.

MIRACULOUSLY, THEY REPEATED THE TRICK THE NEXT YEAR, BEATING HAMBURG 1-0 TO RETAIN THE CUP.

CLOUGH'S STATUS AS ONE OF THE GAME'S GREATS WAS NOW ASSURED.

'THE DAY FOOTBALL DIED'
ITALY 3 BRAZIL 2, 1982

Brazil's first-round performances at the 1982 World Cup had revived memories of their class of 1970, with Sócrates, Zico, Falcão and Cerezo stroking the ball around the centre of the park. With a midfield like that, who needs a competent striker or an organised defence? Having beaten Argentina in the first game of the second group stage, they needed only to draw with Enzo Bearzot's defensively-minded Italy to progress to the semi-finals. The *Azzurri* had been deeply unimpressive in drawing all of their first-round group games, scraping through only by virtue of scoring one more goal than Cameroon.

Everything about Italy v Brazil, however, was a delight to the senses: two great teams wearing classic kits, somehow distinguishable despite not being all the same colour; a sunny Barcelona afternoon illuminating a curiously discoloured pitch; the constant buzz of the spectators' horns; the basic television graphics; the unnecessary visual aid of a pulsating 'R' in the corner of the screen to denote action replays as the goals crashed in; the salty taste of tears as Italy completely ruined everyone's day.

BRAZIL'S PERFORMANCES AT THE PREVIOUS TWO WORLD CUPS HAD BEEN TORPID, BUT TELE SANTANA'S 1982 TEAM WAS FULL OF INDIVIDUAL ATTACKING BRILLIANCE.

Should we practise defending set-pieces today, boss?

Nah.

INJURIES HAD ROBBED THEM OF THEIR FIRST CHOICE STRIKERS, SO SERGINHO LED THE LINE. HE WAS TO BECOME THE MOST MALIGNED FORWARD IN BRAZILIAN FOOTBALL HISTORY. AT LEAST UNTIL 2014.

Thank you.

You're... hurting ...me ...!

FRED

ITALY HAD THEIR OWN PROBLEMS. PAOLO ROSSI HAD BEEN ANONYMOUS IN THEIR PREVIOUS GAMES, HAVING JUST RETURNED FROM A TWO-YEAR BAN FOR MATCH-FIXING; A CHARGE HE STILL DENIED.

I'm telling you, I was set up. It was a one-armed man, see.

Your ball, Paolo!

PAOLO!

Sakes.

20

HOWEVER, IT WAS ROSSI WHO NODDED ITALY INTO AN EARLY LEAD. SÓCRATES LEVELLED, BUT A LOOSE PASS FROM CEREZO PUT IN ROSSI AGAIN TO MAKE IT 2-1. A TEARFUL CEREZO WAS SOOTHED BY HIS TEAM-MATE, JUNIOR.

God damn it, you don't stop crying, I'm gonna smack you in the face.

CEREZO LATER REDEEMED HIMSELF WITH A RUN THAT CREATED SPACE FOR FALCÃO TO EQUALISE, WHICH HE FOLLOWED WITH A GLORIOUSLY SWEATY CELEBRATION.

Antiperspirant deodorant is a construct of the advertising industry!

BRAZIL NOW HAD THE POINT THEY NEEDED, BUT CONTINUED TO ATTACK, WITH PERILOUS CONSEQUENCES.

Everyone get forward! We need to ensure that pundits still paint Brazil as free-flowing football aesthetes for decades after it has ceased to be remotely true!

WITH 15 MINUTES REMAINING, AN ITALIAN CORNER WAS ONLY HALF-CLEARED TO TARDELLI. HIS SCUFFED SHOT WAS TURNED IN BY ROSSI, BEATING THE DECIDEDLY DODGY GOALKEEPER, WALDIR PERES.

The one-armed man !!

BRASIL

Tongo

ITALY'S WINNING POST-CATENACCIO GAMEPLAN WAS A VICTORY FOR TEAMWORK OVER INDIVIDUALITY. BRAZIL NEVER AGAIN PLAYED WITH SUCH ABANDON AND ZICO DESCRIBED IT AS 'THE DAY FOOTBALL DIED'.

A cryin' shame, that's what it is.

BRAZILIAN FREEDOM OF EXPRESSION 1914-1982

THE HIP BONE'S CONNECTED TO THE CHEEK BONE
BATTISTON v SCHUMACHER

The football universe needs balance and, thus, it needs bastards. For every gentlemanly act of charity, there's a scoundrel flicking the Vs at the away end; for every message of social inclusion read out over the PA system, there's a bounder flobbing at a ballboy. As villains go, West Germany's Harald 'Toni' Schumacher was a peach; a wonderful, rotten peach (with a bubble perm and a moustache like a soft porn actor to boot).

Not that the rest of West Germany's 1982 team was packed with saints either. Manager Jupp Derwall had installed a win-at-all-costs mentality which, although successful, earned them few admirers. After conspiring with Austria to achieve a result that would see both teams advance to the second round at the expense of Algeria, there was a mass outcry. Even West Germany's largest tabloid ran with the headline 'SHAME ON YOU!' When a group of disgruntled German fans went to the team hotel to demand an explanation, some of the players pelted them with water balloons. This was truly a special collection of gits.

But surely they would come unstuck in the semi-final against an artful French team? The match was set up perfectly for the forces of light to claim a victory in the name of aesthetics, craft and fair play.

Nope.

THE GAME WAS POISED AT 1-1, BUT FRANCE WERE ON TOP.

THE GERMAN KEEPER, TONI SCHUMACHER, SEEMED FIRED UP. HE'D ALREADY CLASHED WITH PLATINI AND SIX AND THREATENED TO THROW A BALL AT THE FRENCH FANS.

IN THE 57th MINUTE, PLATINI SPLIT THE DEFENCE WITH A PERFECT LOFTED PASS. BATTISTON RACED THROUGH, SCHUMACHER CHARGED OUT. THE BALL BOUNCED ONCE...

AS WORRIED PLAYERS GATHERED ROUND THE PROSTRATE BATTISTON, SCHUMACHER CHOSE TO EXPRESS HIS CONCERN IN A PERSONAL WAY.

Are we taking this goal kick or are we playing the doctors and the nurses?

Amateurs!

BATTISTON LOST THREE TEETH AND LEFT THE FIELD ON A STRETCHER, PLATINI HOLDING HIS LIFELESS HAND. TO HIS CREDIT, SCHUMACHER DID LATER PAY HIM A VISIT.

Hey, if you can't love me at my worst, you don't deserve me at my best. Toffee apple?

Oh yeah, the teeth.

THE GAME ENDED IN A THRILLING 3-3 DRAW, AFTER WHICH THE GERMANS WON THE WORLD CUP'S FIRST EVER PENALTY SHOOT-OUT, THANKS TO TWO SAVES FROM YOU-KNOW-WHO. HOWEVER, THEY WOULD LOSE 3-1 TO ITALY IN THE FINAL.

Why do the bad things always happen to me?!

BATTISTON MADE A FULL RECOVERY, BUT HIS BROKEN TEETH WERE LATER PUT ON DISPLAY IN A BERLIN MUSEUM.

Patrick? Toni. Yeah, that one. Listen, shut up; what are you doing on Saturday? There's an exhibition in Berlin, see...

THE HAND OF GOD
DIEGO MARADONA, 1986

'Oh you horrible little cheat!' 'This is the biggest miscarriage of justice ever to take place on a football field.' 'Something xenophobic about the referee being from Tunisia!'

These are just some of the things people in Buenos Aires were probably saying as Terry Fenwick hacked down Diego Maradona for the umpteenth time during the first half of the World Cup quarter-final between England and Argentina in 1986.

It's fair to say that the two nations had 'history'. Their football rivalry had taken on a bitter edge in the aftermath of Antonio Rattin's sending off at the 1966 World Cup and, on the political front, the two countries had been at war just four years before they met in the heat of the Azteca Stadium in Mexico City.

Both teams had publicly played down the relationship between the sporting rivalry and the war, but away from the microphones it was a different story. In his autobiography *El Diego*, a typically restrained Maradona explains: 'In a way, we blamed the English players for everything that happened, for all the suffering of the Argentine people.'

In a way, *I* blame Steve Hodge's inability to volley a football in its intended direction for everything that followed.

'High noon in Mexico City, the perfect and sensible time to schedule a showdown. For once those FIFA snakes have got something right.'

'But as captain, I have a responsibility to cool the hysteria.'

Football and politics shouldn't mix. This has nothing to do with the Malvinas.

Boys, this has EVERYTHING to do with the Malvinas. Just look at Terry Fenwick with his breakfast DJ hair and tell me he doesn't kiss a picture of Thatcher every night. This is about WAR. This is about REVENGE. THIS IS ABOUT BALLS!

'The first half passes without incident. Bilardo talks to the lads at half-time, but they need to hear from El Diego.'

Blocking their wide players restricts the supply to Beardsl—

BALLS. WAR. REVENGE. BALLS.

'Then my chance. The ball loops in the air from an unconventional Hodge clearance.'

BOING

'Shilton lumbers off his line as if his shorts are filled with guacamole. I have to beat him.'

'Suddenly my mind transports me back to a traumatic childhood memory: falling into the village cesspool in the dead of night. My uncle's voice sings out to me...'

Get your head above the shit!

'But it is easier to just use my hand.'

'God laughs as I pickpocket the English tourists. Justice is mine. I glance back at the referee, but he is distracted.'

It's splash-resistant, tells the time in four zones, it's got a calculator and you can even play Frogger on it.

The English bench is full of fury. They can only stare in wonder at my big balls. Look at my balls, Don Howe. Look at them.'

I don't want to.

THE GOAL OF THE CENTURY
MARADONA'S SECOND

Saudi Arabia's Saeed Al-Owairan collects the ball midway inside his own half. He immediately sets off with a surge of pace, his long legs taking him beyond the centre circle unimpeded. The Belgian defender Medved tries to keep up with him but slumps to the ground with a weak challenge that does nothing to thwart Owairan's progress. He skips outside De Wolf and suddenly Belgium realise the danger. Smidts comes across and is closest to stopping him at the edge of the penalty area, but his tackle is soft and the ball stays within Owairan's reach. Adrenalin pumping, he stretches out and hooks the ball beyond the desperate lunge of Albert and over the advancing goalkeeper Preud'homme. The ball ripples the back of the net and the 50,000 people in the Robert F Kennedy Stadium, Washington, DC, rise as one, having just witnessed the best goal of the 1994, or any other, World Cup.

Eight years before, Diego Maradona had also scored a good goal, against England. Yes, you have to say it was magnificent, but what became of the players he humiliated on that scorching Mexican day?

THE CRAZY GANG VERSUS THE CULTURE CLUB
WIMBLEDON 1 LIVERPOOL 0, 1988

To follow English football in the 1980s was to go on a thrilling rollercoaster ride of wondering how many points Liverpool would win the League by each year. The 1987–88 season was no different, as they claimed the title with five games to spare in a campaign that included a twenty-nine-game unbeaten run. Oh, sweet suspense. The Reds had conceded only one goal on their route to that year's FA Cup final, which would see them making their twenty-first Wembley appearance in fifteen years.

Their unrelenting march of success couldn't even be derailed by the release of perhaps the worst football record of all time, the 'Anfield Rap'. Listening to just one line of Steve McMahon's hip-hop battle with Bruce Grobbelaar induces such a powerful, sphincter-clenching reaction that medical practitioners have been known to prescribe it for some bowel-related complaints.

Talking of the shits, the Wimbledon team they faced that day was owned by Sam Hammam and included Dennis Wise, John Fashanu and Vinnie Jones in the starting line-up. The Dons had just completed their second season in the top flight and had been members of the Football League for only eleven years. As romantic and meteoric as their rise had been, this was Liverpool and no one beat Liverpool.

LIVERPOOL HAD WON THE 1988 LEAGUE TITLE AT A CANTER AND WERE HOT FAVOURITES TO CLAIM ANOTHER DOUBLE.

BUT WIMBLEDON WERE RENOWNED FOR THEIR GREAT TEAM SPIRIT. INDEED, BEING A PART OF THE FAMOUS 'CRAZY GANG' MUST HAVE BEEN A RELENTLESS HOOT!

Oh. Magic. You've torched my car. Again. Great banter, lads.

That's what you get for trying to travel to your place of work, you mug!

LIVERPOOL'S GARY GILLESPIE AND NIGEL SPACKMAN HAD BEEN HOSPITALISED AFTER A CLASH OF HEADS FOUR DAYS EARLIER, BUT WERE PASSED FIT TO PLAY.

How many future TV pundits can you see?

Um, all of them?

You're fine.

WITHIN MOMENTS OF THE KICK-OFF, VINNIE JONES CLATTERED INTO STEVE McMAHON WITH A REDUCER SO LATE THAT THE LIVERPOOL MAN WAS ALREADY WELL INTO HIS DISAPPOINTING MANAGERIAL CAREER BY THE TIME CONTACT WAS MADE.

Perth Glory are a massive club and I'm the man to—

LIVERPOOL WERE DOMINANT BUT IT WAS WIMBLEDON WHO TOOK A SURPRISE 37TH MINUTE LEAD; LAWRIE SANCHEZ RISING ABOVE THE DEFENCE TO DIRECT A LOOPING HEADER INTO THE FAR CORNER.

kippers on a Thursday, Mrs Wizzlethump?!

kneel before your tree king!

IT LOOKED AS IF THE REDS WOULD DRAW LEVEL WHEN THEY WERE AWARDED A SECOND-HALF PENALTY, BUT DAVE BEASANT HAD STUDIED JOHN ALDRIDGE'S SPOT-KICK TECHNIQUE AND DIVED TO HIS LEFT TO SAVE IT.

There are some benefits to Liverpool being on the TV every Sunday.

THE UNDERDOGS HELD ON FOR A FAMOUS WIN. MANY OF THE SQUAD WENT ON TO EVEN GREATER THINGS, INCLUDING VINNIE JONES, WHO WOULD ESTABLISH HIMSELF AS A CHAMELEON-LIKE CHARACTER ACTOR.

HENCHMAN   HOOLIGAN   ENFORCER   GOON (UNCREDITED)

THE WIN PUT 'THE DONS' ON THE FOOTBALL MAP. IT ALSO MEANT THAT YEARS LATER, WHEN PLANS WERE AFOOT TO MOVE THE CLUB TO MILTON KEYNES, STRIPPING THEM OF THEIR WHOLE IDENTITY, THE FOOTBALL AUTHORITIES PROVIDED UNEQUIVOCAL RESISTANCE.

Hah, yeah, go on then.

FROM PERIMETER ROPE TO GIGANTIC SLOPES
THE EVOLUTION OF THE BRITISH FOOTBALL STADIUM

The twenty-first-century British football stadium is a wonder of steel and glass and primary-coloured bucket seats. Unless you're a steward or a cleaner it's unlikely you'll ever be able to go inside, but you've seen them on the telly, so know they're probably nice.

In recent times, football has become inaccessible to vast swathes of people. This is for the best: the top clubs didn't go through weeks of painstaking negotiations over stadium naming-rights only to admit the likes of you. Those plastic seats might look wipe-clean but mustard stains are a bugger to remove.

If you can't afford to access the exclusive VIP area of the Premier League, you could always look further down the football pyramid. You'll find new stadiums there, too, but their identikit designs could be mistaken for out-of-town garden centres. Want a pointless Buddha statue for your back decking? Toddle on down to the Keepmoat Stadium. Need a fire pit to really make that high-rise balcony pop? Get yourself to the Madejski.

These stadiums might not draw admiring gasps from the design community but they are at least safe. For decades before, British football stadiums remained frozen in time, fossilised relics of a bygone era where people gathered to drink Bovril.

'IT'S UP FOR GRABS NOW!'
LIVERPOOL 0 ARSENAL 2, 1989

Friday 26 May 1989. A mild, spring evening. The last match of the season, a genuine title-decider. Liverpool, in pole position, hosting Arsenal – second placed and needing to win by a two-goal margin to overhaul the leaders. Get the kettle on and unplug the phone (you still have a landline, it's 1989).

Arsenal had led the League for most of the season and were fifteen points ahead of Liverpool in January, but their form dropped badly as Liverpool went on their annual unbeaten run (eighteen matches this time). Liverpool finally leapfrogged Arsenal in mid-May with wins against QPR and West Ham, while Arsenal could amass just a solitary point from fixtures with Derby County and Wimbledon. If Arsenal Fan TV had existed then, it would have melted the internet a mile into the ground.

Liverpool had not lost by two goals or more at Anfield in three years and Arsenal hadn't won there in fifteen. Liverpool were also undefeated when Ian Rush and John Aldridge played together. The omens for George Graham's side weren't good.

However, there was another factor at play: the match was taking place just six weeks after so many Liverpool fans had lost their lives at Hillsborough and just days after Liverpool had won a physically and emotionally draining FA Cup final against Everton. It was understandable if their minds were on weightier issues than tracking the runs of Martin Hayes.

THE LAST TIME ARSENAL HAD WON THE LEAGUE, IN 1971, GEORGE GRAHAM WAS A CREATIVE PLAYER SO LANGUID THAT HE WAS NICKNAMED 'STROLLER'.

GEORGE!

Yeah, after this.

HOWEVER, HIS APPROACH AS A MANAGER WAS VERY DIFFERENT.

Perry! If you don't align those sock turnovers, you'll be polishing my blazer buttons until your fingers atomise.

HIS WELL-DRILLED SIDE HAD SUFFERED A LOSS OF FORM, THOUGH, AND THAT DAY'S DAILY MIRROR BELLOWED: 'YOU HAVEN'T GOT A PRAYER, ARSENAL.'

FUTURE ARSENAL-SUPPORTING MIRROR EDITORS WOULD SHARE THIS OPTIMISTIC OUTLOOK.

We didn't sign Messi OR Ronaldo! Is there any group of people who have suffered more than Arsenal fans?

AFTER A CAUTIOUS FIRST HALF, ALAN SMITH HEADED THE GUNNERS INTO A 57TH MINUTE LEAD. THE ARSENAL BENCH ERUPTS.

Never mind that, keep polishing those buttons, laddie.

AS THE GAME MOVED INTO STOPPAGE TIME, STEVE McMAHON MISTAKENLY TOLD HIS TEAM-MATES THAT THEY ONLY HAD TO HANG ON FOR ONE MINUTE. AT HOME, A YOUNG STEVEN GERRARD TOOK NOTE.

You'll never see me tempting fate like that.

THEN, WITH SECONDS REMAINING, LEE DIXON'S LUNG BALL WAS HELPED ON BY SMITH AND MICHAEL THOMAS FOUND HIMSELF IN THE PENALTY BOX WITH ONLY THE KEEPER TO BEAT.

IT'S UP FOR GRABS NOW...!

ONCE HE'D LIFTED THE BALL OVER GROBBELAAR AND INTO THE REDS' NET, THOMAS WAS SO ECSTATIC THAT HE DIDN'T KNOW WHAT TO DO WITH HIMSELF. SO HE DID THIS:

UNDER THE CIRCUMSTANCES THIS WAS AN ENTIRELY REASONABLE REACTION.

ARSENAL HAD DONE IT, SENDING THEIR FANS WILD WITH JOY.

We haven't won the league in three minutes! When will the spineless Arsenal board sack the inept George Graham?!

LIVERPOOL'S FANS DIDN'T LEAVE OR BOO; THEY STOOD AND APPLAUDED THE NEW CHAMPIONS AND THEIR OWN BRAVE TEAM. AFTER ALL, IT'S ONLY FOOTBALL.

A SHOE SALESMAN'S GRAND PLAN
ARRIGO SACCHI'S MILAN

Before Arrigo Sacchi's arrival at AC Milan in 1987, Italian football was, unimaginably, regarded as being low-scoring and cautious. Sacchi had a vision: to change that perception and create an elegant passing-team for the ages. If there was one man capable of fulfilling the aspirations of a bright young starlet, it was Milan owner Silvio Berlusconi.

The once great Milan had fallen into decline. In the early eighties they even dropped down to Serie B a couple of times; first, for involvement in a betting scandal, and second, for being a bit hopeless at football. Although they had returned to the top flight, even the presence of players of the quality of Luther Blissett and Mark Hateley couldn't bring them success. Their shirt sponsors at the time hinted at their status as the players would trot out on to the San Siro turf with the words 'Pooh jeans' spread across the famous red and black shirts.

When the media mogul Berlusconi became president of the *Rossoneri* in early 1986, he brought money, influence and hope. With Sacchi employed as coach, Milan would re-establish themselves as one of the giants of European football. Together, they would put the grand old club on a path that would eventually lead to a dance troupe in Milan shirts performing a haka in front of a bewildered home crowd as part of a publicity stunt to advertise moisturising cream. The stuff that dreams are made of.

ARRIGO SACCHI WAS A FORMER SHOE SALESMAN WHO DREAMED OF COACHING A TEAM TO EMULATE THE GREAT PASSING SIDES OF THE AGES.

Hoo boy, it's good to get some cool air on that bunion.

HE MADE A NAME FOR HIMSELF IN THE ITALIAN LOWER LEAGUES AND IT WAS WHILE COACHING PARMA THAT HE CAUGHT THE EYE OF MILAN OWNER, SILVIO BERLUSCONI, WHO SOON OFFERED HIM THE MANAGER'S JOB.

How could you refuse this face?

SACCHI NEVER PLAYED PROFESSIONALLY, BUT WHEN HIS CREDENTIALS WERE QUESTIONED, HE POINTED OUT THAT YOU DON'T NEED TO HAVE BEEN A HORSE IN ORDER TO BE A JOCKEY.

Solid point.

MILAN WON THE SCUDETTO IN HIS FIRST YEAR. THE TEAM WAS MADE UP OF LOCAL TALENT AND DUTCH BRILLIANCE.

That one freaks me out, man. The way he looks at me, like he sees through me.

VAN BASTEN

GULLIT

RIJKAARD

TASSOTTI

ANCELOTTI

COSTACURTA

BARESI

MALDINI

DONADONI

That's just Ancelotti, he's all right.

Really...? I dunno...

A TRAINING INNOVATION OF SACCHI'S WAS TO GET THE SQUAD TO PLAY A FULL MATCH WITHOUT A BALL; SOMETHING STEAUA BUCHAREST EXPERIENCED WHEN MILAN THUMPED THEM 4-0 TO WIN THE 1989 EUROPEAN CUP FINAL.

Ooh, it's heavy, but it's so pretty.

Good, good.

THEY RETAINED THE TROPHY THE FOLLOWING YEAR, BEATING BENFICA 1-0 IN THE FINAL. HOWEVER, SACCHI WAS FIRED IN 1991 AFTER A PLAYER DISPUTE.

Well, the last thing I expected from Dutch internationals was self-destructive conflict.

REGARDLESS, HE REMAINED WIDELY-RESPECTED RIGHT UP TO THE POINT WHERE HE SHAT ON HIS LEGACY FROM THE HEIGHT OF THE SAN SIRO BY SAYING THERE WERE TOO MANY BLACK PLAYERS IN ITALY'S YOUTH SET UP.

I'm not a racist, but gfnfnkhnf...

THE INDOMITABLE LIONS
ARGENTINA 0 CAMEROON 1, 1990

For years the presence of African teams at World Cup finals was viewed as a curiosity. At best, commentators would patronise them, expressing surprise that a group of people who had apparently stepped directly from the pages of *National Geographic* were somehow able to trap a football. Sides were often described as being 'naïve' and frequent references were made to witch doctors, as if team selections were based on the random scattering of chicken bones.

When Cameroon stormed to the quarter-finals of the 1990 World Cup some of these attitudes began to change, although in the ITV commentary box Ron Atkinson still found time to wonder whether Benjamin Massing's mother had been watching the game 'up a tree'. He definitely wasn't a racist, though. After all, when he was West Brom manager he had employed black players to follow his commands and even nicknamed them the Three Degrees, which they no doubt loved.

Inspired by the goals of octogenarian striker Roger Milla, Cameroon's collection of journeymen from the French lower leagues took Italia '90 by storm. Their amazing run began at the San Siro with a shock 1–0 win against reigning champions Argentina, François Omam-Biyik's header squirming past Nery Pumpido on the line.

However, there was a physical side to their game, which sometimes crossed the line into all-out violence. Already reduced to ten men, the Cameroon team set off in pursuit of Claudio Caniggia, who was racing up-field in search of an equaliser...

'HAVE A WORD WITH HIM'
PAUL GASCOIGNE, 1990

Footballers didn't cry in public, not English ones anyway. We were used to seeing stiff upper lips, not quivering lower ones. Yet here we were in 1990, in extra-time of a World Cup semi-final, and the player who had lit up England's tournament was expressing real human emotion. We didn't get this with Trevor Steven.

England fell in love with Paul Gascoigne during the summer of 1990. His skill and drive and exuberance inspired the team to go further than they had in decades. Although England fans were devastated to lose that semi-final on penalties to West Germany, for once there was hope. Here was a young player who would surely mature into one of the finest players in the world. Watch out, USA '94!

Of course, the 250,000 people who turned up at Luton Airport to greet the returning England team – and specifically 'Gazza' – had no idea that this weight of expectation would crush him like a pair of plastic comedy breasts under the wheels of an open-top bus. Gazzamania swept the nation. He appeared on chat shows, released records, produced merchandise and advertised just about every product you could imagine. Sadly, behind the grinning affability was a troubled and flawed human being.

ENGLAND FANS ARE RENOWNED FOR THEIR LEVEL-HEADEDNESS WHEN A YOUNG PROSPECT SHOWS TALENT.

Shaun Wright-Phillips is the new Puskás!

Jack Wilshere is the new Hagi!

Andros Townsend is the new Shaun Wright-Phillips!

SO IMAGINE THEIR EXCITEMENT WHEN ONE OF THE WORLD'S MOST EXCITING PLAYERS WAS WEARING AN ENGLAND SHIRT.

PAUL GASCOIGNE WAS DYNAMIC, HYPERACTIVE, TROUBLED AND, ON HIS DAY, BRILLIANT. BUT BEFORE THE 1990 WORLD CUP, ENGLAND MANAGER BOBBY ROBSON HAD RESERVATIONS ABOUT HIS DISCIPLINE, DESCRIBING HIM AS BEING 'AS DAFT AS A BRUSH'.

WILD! WACKY! SCREWY! ZANY! PROPENSITY TO FILL CHRIS WADDLE'S SLIP-ONS WITH DOG FOOD!

ENGLAND'S OPENING MATCH AGAINST IRELAND RAN TRUE TO FORM, WITH A TURGID DRAW. HOWEVER, A MUCH-IMPROVED PERFORMANCE AGAINST THE NETHERLANDS WAS INSPIRED BY THE ENERGY AND DRIVE OF GASCOIGNE. AT ONE POINT HE EVEN EXECUTED A CRUYFF-LIKE TURN TO SKIP AWAY FROM RONALD KOEMAN.

HE THEN PLAYED A KEY ROLE IN THE WINS AGAINST EGYPT, BELGIUM AND CAMEROON TO SET UP A SEMI-FINAL WITH WEST GERMANY. THE GAME WOULD CHANGE HIS LIFE AND HE PREPARED FOR IT BY PLAYING TENNIS AGAINST SOME AMERICAN TOURISTS.

LAWN TENNIS ASSOCIATION, LONDON

Sir, we're getting unconfirmed reports that an English male has won a tennis match.

ENGLAND FOUGHT HARD, NONE MORE SO THAN GASCOIGNE, BUT A RECKLESS LUNGE ON THOMAS BERTHOLD EARNED HIM A YELLOW CARD, MEANING HE WOULD BE UNABLE TO PLAY IN THE FINAL SHOULD ENGLAND PROGRESS. AS HIS EYES FILLED WITH HOT TEARS, GARY LINEKER ADVISED THE BENCH TO 'HAVE A WORD WITH HIM'.

I'm no psychologist, but I suspect his issues may be more complex than mere football-related matters...

PERHAPS GASCOIGNE'S LIFE WOULD HAVE BEEN LESS CHAOTIC IF LINEKER HAD BEEN FORCED TO STAY BY HIS SIDE AT ALL TIMES...

There's a killer on the loose, so I just thought I'd pop down and give him some chicken and cans.

Please let me stop.

AT THE END OF EXTRA-TIME, BEFORE THE PENALTY SHOOT-OUT THAT ENGLAND WOULD LOSE, ROBSON CONSOLED A TEARFUL GASCOIGNE. HIS WORDS ARE CAPTURED IN THE FILM 'ONE NIGHT IN TURIN' AND SHOULD COME WITH SOME SORT OF WARNING.

Don't worry, son. You've been absolutely magnificent, haven't you, yeah?

You've got your whole life ahead of you.

This is your first. Don't worry about it.

FOOTBALL BECOMES TRENDY
SELL YOUR ORGANS FOR
A CATEGORY F TICKET

For decades football supporters were dehumanised, herded, prodded, insulted, beaten, killed. This contempt for human life permeated through governments, police forces, newspapers and the very chairmen and directors of the football clubs we supported. Truly, football fans were the enemy within.

In the early 1990s, football in Britain began to change. England had enjoyed a successful World Cup in Italy, with the focus more on events on the field than in the streets. There was a new, unfamiliar positivity about the game. The Taylor Report had heralded a flurry of redevelopments, as clubs finally accepted their responsibilities to drag their facilities into the twentieth century.

Suddenly, football was the place to be seen, especially if you wanted to promote your credentials as a grounded man of the people. There was also money to be made.

One of the great ironies about the gentrification of football was that the media organisation that had spread hateful lies about the events at Hillsborough would soon own most of English football's broadcasting rights. The game was rebranded and sold back to us at a premium.

Monstrous TV deals meant more money for the clubs, but that money slid directly through to players and their agents. As the clubs got richer, the price of tickets continued to soar. The average price of a Premier League ticket in 1992 was £8. Allowing for inflation, this would be around £15.50 in 2016, or about the cost of a stadium pie.

IN THE 1980s, BEING A FOOTBALL FAN WAS HAZARDOUS. THE GROUNDS WERE DEATH TRAPS, HOOLIGANISM WAS RIFE AND SUPPORTERS WERE SOCIAL PARIAHS.

Those monsters should be on some sort of register.

BUT A NUMBER OF FACTORS CHANGED THE SITUATION IN THE DECADE THAT FOLLOWED. THE TAYLOR REPORT LED TO SAFER, MORE COMFORTABLE STADIUMS.

Women's toilets?! I wanted to stick a fruit platter in that cupboard and market it as an executive suite. Bloody feminists!

AND DESPITE THE OFTEN DULL FOOTBALL, ITALIA '90 GRIPPED THE NATION, DRAWING HUGE TELEVISION AUDIENCES.

Another textbook backpass from Uruguay, Trevor...

CROWD VIOLENCE ABATED. THIS HAS SOMETIMES BEEN EXPLAINED BY THE EMERGENCE OF RAVE CULTURE AND ITS ASSOCIATED SUBSTANCES. THE DRUG REVOLUTION PASSED SOME OF US BY, THOUGH.

THE QUEUE FOR CAIROS NIGHTCLUB, SWINDON, EARLY 1990s

This raspberry-flavoured fortified wine is blowing my mind!

IMPORTANTLY, THE CREATION OF THE PREMIER LEAGUE ALSO CAME WITH THE ASSOCIATED HYPE THAT THE FOOTBALL CLOCK HAD BEEN RE-SET.

This is Year One. Your re-education continues with QPR v Ipswich after this short break.

SUDDENLY IT WAS FASHIONABLE TO BE A FAN, WITH CELEBRITIES AND POLITICIANS CLAMOURING TO BE SPOTTED AT MATCHES.

Wow, was that her off breakfast telly?

Yep, and she's with that minister who wanted to birch all season ticket holders four years ago.

PLAYERS CHANGED TOO. MODERN IDEAS ABOUT CONDITIONING SAW TERRIFYING MOUSTACHIOED MEN REPLACED WITH MUSCULAR MALE-MODEL ATHLETES.

THIS TRANSITION WAS NOT IMMEDIATE

COVENTRY CITY

MICK QUINN

BY THE TIME ENGLAND HOSTED EURO 96, IT WAS COMPULSORY FOR EVERY CITIZEN TO BE A SELF-CONFESSED FOOTIE NUT!

That pervert's not even wearing the new England top. In broad daylight!

ALTHOUGH THIS POPULARITY LED TO MANY BEING PRICED OUT OF THE GAME, UNABLE TO WATCH IN THE STADIUMS OR ON PAY TV, SOLUTIONS WERE AT HAND.

OK, I've found a blocky live stream. The commentary is in Mandarin, but you can make out the players if you close one eye.

'BLOW THEM OUT OF THE WATER'
THE FORMATION OF THE PREMIER LEAGUE

Before the formation of the Premier League, money was distributed evenly throughout the four divisions of the Football League, nourishing the game's grass roots and helping to keep the sport competitive.

Clearly, this breeding ground of anti-capitalist wealth-hate had to change. Let the free market decide which communities see their football clubs wither and die. This isn't Albania, pinkos!

The genesis of the Premier League came from the managing director of London Weekend Television, Greg Dyke. Displaying a comprehension of the history and culture of English football that would later serve him well as FA chairman, Dyke believed that it would be better if only the big clubs were televised. He approached the 'Big Five' of Manchester United, Liverpool, Arsenal, Tottenham and Everton (Everton!) to see if they would be interested in receiving a bigger slice of TV money. This meeting – probably the shortest in history – paved the way for a defection from the Football League.

The challenge they faced was enlisting the support of the Football Association. Indeed, they had to wait a matter of minutes before the governing body – responsible for representing the interests of all clubs, regardless of size – rolled over on to its back and begged to have its tummy scratched.

The FA's subsequent *Blueprint for the Future of Football* sanctioned the move, claiming it would be beneficial to the national team. The fact that England have never again got as far in the World Cup as in the year before the publication of that plan is immaterial. It's only been a quarter of a century, you have to think long term, yeah.

With the new Premier League set to launch in the 1992–93 season, all that was now needed was a broadcasting deal.

THE BROADCASTING RIGHTS FOR THE NEWLY FORMED PREMIER LEAGUE ARE UP FOR GRABS. AS THE BIDDERS GATHER AT A LONDON HOTEL, THE DEBATE HOTS UP...

Listen, you wallies, the world is changing. In the future, punters won't even watch football on the telly; they'll watch it on their phones.

Phones made by me!

GET THE BIG MATCH FAXED LIVE! FRAME BY FRAME

£399.99

It's even better than being there!

Come off it, Alan; there's a clear conflict of interest here. You're the chairman of Spurs and you make the satellite dishes for Murdoch's flailing empire.

'Flailing'? You mug, I bet ITV or the BBC couldn't build one of them...

FOX NEWS

Regardless, our bid at ITV is £262 million. I sincerely doubt anyone can match that.

Hold up, I've gotta see a man about a dog.

Blow them out of the water!

Prepare the laser cannon, Commander.

Um, I think he was speaking metaphorically, My Lord...

The cannon, Commander.

AND SO, FOR THE FIRST TIME, PEOPLE IN BRITAIN WOULD HAVE TO PAY A SUBSCRIPTION TO WATCH TELEVISED TOP-FLIGHT FOOTBALL. THE DEAL ALSO MEANT PERMANENT FINANCIAL SECURITY FOR THE BREAKAWAY CLUBS (INCLUDING WIMBLEDON, OLDHAM, LUTON AND SHEFFIELD UNITED). NATURALLY, THE GUARDIANS OF THE GAME, THE FA, WERE AT HAND TO ENSURE THAT THE ETHICS OF THE SPORT WERE UPHELD AND THAT THE FOOTBALL PYRAMID WOULD IN NO WAY BE COMPROMISED.

Anything you want to add here, Graham? You know, as FA chief exec...?

Can't. Tetris.

SUPER SUBS
DENMARK WIN EURO 92

The popular myth about the Danish team that won the 1992 European Championship in Sweden is that they were 'on the beach' when they discovered that they would be taking part in the tournament, replacing Yugoslavia.

While the beaches of Denmark are beautiful, with crystal blue waters and soft white sand, Danish crime dramas have taught us that they are also littered with socially dysfunctional detectives studying the remains of creatively dismembered murder victims. They are no place for an international football team. It's true that Richard Møller Nielsen had very little time to ready his team, but they were already in Sweden, where they were due to play a friendly against the Commonwealth of Independent States.

Not that this diminishes their achievement. For a small nation to arrive at a major tournament at such short notice and then see off the likes of France, Holland and Germany requires a stretch of the imagination even beyond that asked of us by the producers of a Scandinavian crime noir series.

LITTLE WAS EXPECTED OF DENMARK AT EURO 92. THEY WERE A HARD-WORKING TEAM, BUT LIVED IN THE SHADOW OF THEIR SUBLIME SIDE OF THE 1980s, WHICH BOASTED AN ARRAY OF TALENT AND ONE OF THE BEST KITS OF ALL TIME.

To be fair, you're all living in the shadow of this.

PLUS, RICHARD MØLLER NIELSEN HAD LITTLE OVER A WEEK TO PREPARE HIS TEAM TO FACE GRAHAM TAYLOR'S ENGLAND.

I've done all I can for them. Now they must face Andy Sinton alone.

Boss, they've picked Keith Curle at right-back....!

What tactical wizardry is this?

SOMEHOW THEY MANAGED. AFTER NEGOTIATING THE GROUP STAGE, DENMARK FACED A HOLLAND TEAM WHO SEEMED PRE-OCCUPIED BY THE PROSPECT OF A SHOWDOWN WITH ARCH-RIVALS GERMANY IN THE FINAL.

I hold Guido Buchwald personally responsible for the theft of my grandfather's bicycle during the war. I will have my vengeance.

HOLLAND TREATED THE GAME AS AN INCONVENIENT HURDLE AND THE DANES WERE ANGERED TO SEE THAT THEY BARELY CELEBRATED THEIR FIRST GOAL.

I'm sorry, but if there's one thing I don't expect from the Dutch national team, it's arrogance.

Headers and volleys for the next goal?

Heh, ok.

THE DUTCH PAID FOR THEIR COMPLACENCY. AFTER A 2-2 DRAW, DENMARK WON ON PENALTIES.

IN THE FINAL, THEY WITHSTOOD A BARRAGE OF EARLY PRESSURE FROM GERMANY. PETER SCHMEICHEL MADE SOME VITAL SAVES, USING HIS NATURAL ABILITY TO APPEAR LARGE WHEN THREATENED.

I'm in!

SKREEEEEEE

God, I hope that's ink.

Hope what you like, mate.

THEN THE UNIMAGINABLE: A LONG-RANGE MISSILE FROM JOHN JENSEN PUT DENMARK AHEAD. THE GOAL WAS ENOUGH TO EARN THE BRØNDBY MIDFIELDER A TRANSFER TO ARSENAL.

I'm delighted to introduce our new signing, who I'm assuming scores goals like that every week.

A LATE GOAL FROM KIM VILFORT ASSURED DENMARK OF VICTORY. EVEN THEIR OWN PLAYERS SEEMED SURPRISED AT WHAT THEY HAD ACHIEVED.

Sorry. Overexcited.

POWER TO THE PLUTOCRATS!
THE CREATION OF THE CHAMPIONS LEAGUE

The European Cup was an uncomplicated competition: the top team from each country played in a straight knockout tournament to decide who the best side in Europe was. Naturally, the bigger clubs from the wealthiest leagues usually prevailed, but there always existed the chance that a well-managed team with a talented pool of players and a bit of luck could upset Europe's elite. In the 1980s alone, winners included Nottingham Forest, Aston Villa, PSV Eindhoven, Porto, Hamburg and Steaua Bucharest. This kind of bullshit was clearly unacceptable.

'It's nonsense that a club of Milan's standing should be eliminated in the first round of the European Cup,' honked Milan president Silvio Berlusconi to widespread agreement from other wealthy club owners.

Faced with the threat of the powerful clubs breaking up with them, UEFA folded to their every demand, knowing this would surely win their respect. The European Cup was restructured to guarantee more revenue for the top clubs and the newly named Champions League came into effect in the 1992–93 season. Milan were defeated in the final by Marseille, who were later stripped of their title after a match-fixing scandal involving their former owner, Bernard Tapie.

The Champions League has more recently entered an exciting new period, where variety comes in the form of seeing which team will claim a semi-final spot alongside Real Madrid, Barcelona and Bayern Munich. Yet, everything is never quite enough for Europe's football aristocracy; their insatiable hunger for power and wealth has seen them press for closed membership of the competition, with entry requirements primarily being related to financial influence.

It'll be a while before a team from Romania lift the trophy again.

AS EUROPE'S ELITE CLUBS AGITATE FOR CHANGE, UEFA CHAIRMAN LENNART JOHANSSON IS FACED WITH THE THREAT OF A BREAKAWAY. HE MEETS WITH AC MILAN OWNER SILVIO BERLUSCONI TO SHARE HIS GRAND VISION FOR A NEWLY FORMED 'CHAMPIONS LEAGUE'.

So you see, by centralising our commercial activities, an increase in revenue will be guaranteed. Exclusive TV rights will be sold in each country and blue chip businesses will clamour to advertise their beer and tyres and gas extraction through our competition.

Everyone likes gas extraction, Lennart; but it's nonsense that a club of Milan's standing should face the prospect of elimination from the bunga party over something as trivial as losing a football match.

We'll introduce a group stage! You'll get extra earnings from at least three home matches and the risk of elimination will be minimised.

Now you're thinking. You'll need more teams, though.

Europe is changing, growing. The newly independent states will provide more than enough clubs to—

If I wanted to experience the majesty of Belarus, I'd have it shipped to my summer house at Lake Como!

No, you need to increase the number of competitors from the biggest leagues. A club that finishes fourth in Serie A shouldn't be excluded on account of some twisted meritocracy.

Hah, yes, but then it wouldn't be a 'champions' league'...

You're going to force the break up of European club football over a fucking apostrophe, Lennart?

Well, if you put it like that...

Better. Now, this business of having to actually 'qualify'. Correct me if I'm wrong, but I thought communism had been defeated...

Um. Did I tell you about the anthem?

SUNSHINE AND SHELL SUITS
USA '94

It was the best of World Cups (Baggio, Hagi, Romário), it was the worst of World Cups (Escobar, Maradona, Norway). Without generalising, it was a World Cup that coincided with us all being art students and therefore not faced with the usual challenge of avoiding work or school or our cousin Chris's wedding in order to watch the matches.

With the British nations all opting to watch the tournament from home, too, we could relax knowing it was safe to pop the kettle on at half-time and not miss a thrilling update from the England camp. For the first couple of weeks of the competition perhaps you chose to reinforce your Irish credentials through the drinking of stout and the casual use of the phrase 'yer man...' Once Ireland had been knocked out, you were free to pick another side.

The tournament was mostly played in sunshine so bright that it seemed atom bombs were being tested in the stadium car parks. Tuning in to the late-night broadcasts was like stepping out of a cinema into broad daylight. The timing of those matches created a naturally calm atmosphere in the TV studios, as if Bob Wilson was presenting *The Late Show*. Watching football at that hour was a real novelty, especially since, as we have established, you were an art student and therefore blissfully devoid of responsibility.

A BUNCH OF REASONS WHY USA '94 WAS FRIKKIN' AWESOME

ROMANIANS!

BULGARIANS!

THE TENSION CREATED BY THE FEELING THAT ALEXI LALAS COULD REACH FOR AN ACOUSTIC GUITAR AT ANY MOMENT.

Guys, gather round. Cobi, get those s'mores on the campfire. We all know the words to 'What's Up' by 4 Non Blondes?

JOHN ALDRIDGE INTRODUCING A GLOBAL AUDIENCE TO THE RICHNESS OF THE ENGLISH LANGUAGE DURING AN EXCHANGE WITH A FIFA JOBSWORTH.

Fock off, yew! Yer twat! Yer fockin' dick 'ed!

DIANA ROSS MISSING A PENALTY DURING THE OPENING CEREMONY.

This must be a new FIFA directive: even if you miss, everyone has to celebrate. I must tell Baresi.

NIGERIA'S RASHIDI YEKINI GOING NUTS IN THE GOAL NET AFTER SCORING AGAINST BULGARIA.

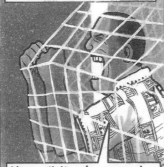

How will this tournament survive without the presence of Graham Taylor's England?!

BEBETO'S 'ROCKING CRADLE' GOAL CELEBRATION, WHICH WAS ORIGINAL AND CUTE AT THE TIME AND LACKED THE POWER TO MAKE YOU FEEL OLD UPON DISCOVERING THAT HIS BABY SON NOW LOOKS LIKE THIS:

FOR EUROPEANS, STAYING UP UNTIL THE EARLY HOURS TO WATCH A GOALLESS DRAW BETWEEN SOUTH KOREA AND BOLIVIA.

We dodged a bullet here, Graham. These two look tidy.

THE DRUGS WERE JUST RESTING IN MY BLOODSTREAM
MARADONA'S DOWNFALL

Nothing about Diego Maradona's character or general behaviour suggested a long-term dependency on cocaine. After all, just a year before he tested positive for the drug, he had captained Argentina to the 1990 World Cup final in Italy. During that tournament he demanded that his hotel balcony be permanently filled with fresh flowers and would listen to Lambada mix tapes at full volume all day. His two Ferraris were parked on the gravel outside the team hotel and he spent $60,000 on a training machine called an 'isokinetic ergometer' (he probably shouldn't have been allowed access to the home shopping channel). He also had his own masseuse (Monica) as well as specially prepared meat from his own barbecue chef. Nope, no clues there as to an addiction to an ego-inflating narcotic.

His Napoli career ruined, Maradona returned home to Buenos Aires to see out his suspension, dusting off the old isokinetic ergometer and working to get fit for the 1994 World Cup. He made his comeback for Argentina in a play-off win against Australia that ensured qualification. Diego was back and determined to take the World Cup by storm. Florists of America, be prepared.

IN 1991, DIEGO MARADONA RECEIVED A 15-MONTH BAN FOR COCAINE USE. HE LATER ADMITTED THAT HE'D BEEN TAKING COCAINE SINCE 1982, EVEN WHILE APPEARING IN ANTI-DRUG CAMPAIGNS.

HE RETURNED TO BUENOS AIRES AND WORKED HARD TO GET FIT, BUT CONTROVERSY WAS NEVER FAR AWAY. IN FEBRUARY 1994 HE WAS FILMED SHOOTING AT REPORTERS WITH AN AIR PISTOL.

Say hello to my little friend!

PYEW

OW! That really hurt!

That tired Scarface parody is only getting two stars now.

STILL, HE MADE IT TO THE WORLD CUP AND WAS INSTRUMENTAL IN ARGENTINA'S 4-0 DEMOLITION OF GREECE. AFTER SCORING A GOAL, HE RAN SCREAMING TO THE TOUCHLINE TV CAMERA.

Hm. Which player should we drug test after Argentina's next match?

MARADONA THEN PLAYED A KEY ROLE IN ARGENTINA'S WIN AGAINST NIGERIA, BUT A FEW DAYS LATER NEWS BROKE THAT HE'D FAILED A DOPE TEST AND HAD BEEN THROWN OUT OF THE WORLD CUP. HE MAINTAINS THAT HIS PERSONAL TRAINER HAD MISTAKENLY GIVEN HIM THE WRONG SUPPLEMENTS.

RIPPED FAST

RIPPED FUEL

Tomayto, tomarto.

IT WOULD APPEAR HE HAS A STRONG CASE. AS HE EXPLAINS IN HIS AUTOBIOGRAPHY:

I was given ephedrine and ephedrine is legal,

or at least it ought to be.

HE SPENT THE REST OF THE WORLD CUP WORKING IN THE COMMENTARY BOX FOR ARGENTINIAN TV.

IT WAS A SAD END TO THE INTERNATIONAL CAREER OF THE GREATEST PLAYER OF ALL TIME.

Do we drug test the media industry?

Don't be ridiculous. I hardly think there'd be so much moralising about drug use if they were all ripped to the tits at every opportunity.

THE MURDER OF
ANDRÉS ESCOBAR
COLOMBIA, 1994

Colombia's talented team had caught the attention of the world with a 5–0 destruction of Argentina in Buenos Aires during qualifying. Expectations were now raised as to how the team would perform at the World Cup. Among those who were whipped along with this wave of excitement were the powerful drug cartels who had dragged Colombia into a state of murderous anarchy. They bet heavily on Colombia being successful.

Reality bit with a 3–1 defeat to Romania in their opening game at the tournament. They now needed a good result against the United States to avoid elimination. On the day of the match, coach Francisco Maturana and midfielder Gabriel Gómez received telephoned death threats.

Colombia started well, driven by the consequences of failure, but in the thirty-fourth minute the rock of their defence, Andrés Escobar, stretched out a leg to cut out a cross and inadvertently steered the ball into his own net. For a moment he lay still, staring up at the sky. The US would go on to win 2–1 and Colombia were out.

Some of the players who returned to Colombia faced intimidation but Escobar, the captain, was widely respected. The Colombian press had savaged the team but applauded Escobar for returning home. On Friday 1 July, he decided to go out for an evening for the first time since his return to Medellín. He was in a nightclub when a group of people began insulting him. He left but the group followed him. He got into his car but made the fatal decision to drive back across the car park to speak to the group. At this point he was shot six times and killed. Humberto Castro Muñoz, a bodyguard for the notorious Gallón cartel, later confessed to the murder and was imprisoned for forty-three years (but released after eleven for good behaviour).

Shortly before his murder, Escobar had written the opposite words in his regular column for Bogotá's *El Tiempo* newspaper.

'Life does not end here. We have to go on...

Life cannot end here...

No matter how difficult, we must stand back up...

We have only two options: either allow anger to paralyse us and the violence continues...

or we overcome and try our best to help others...

It's our choice...

Let us please maintain respect...

My warmest regards to everyone. It's been a most amazing and rare experience...

We'll see each other again soon, because life does not end here.

'OFF YOU GO, CANTONA. IT'S AN EARLY SHOWER FOR YOU!'
ERIC CANTONA'S KUNG-FU KICK

In February 1992 Leeds United manager Howard Wilkinson signed the supremely talented forward Eric Cantona, presumably after bonding over a mutual love of French surrealist poetry. Cantona inspired Leeds to the League title that season, but the relationship between player and manager later broke down and he was dropped.

Sniffing an opportunity, Alex Ferguson made a speculative bid of £1 million to sign him for Manchester United. To his surprise Wilkinson accepted. The bid had taken place during a negotiation about the transfer of another player. We will never know if Carl Shutt would have helped Manchester United to four Premier League trophies in the next five years, but Cantona did.

Despite his undoubted talent, the rebellious Cantona had a problem with authority, as denoted by the wearing of his collar in the up position. His poor disciplinary record merely added to his cult status. He had received a four-match European ban for scrapping with Turkish policemen after a red card at Galatasaray, been fined for spitting at a Leeds fan, kicked a Norwich player in the head, stamped on a Swindon player's chest and received a five-game suspension for being sent off in consecutive matches. He wasn't a man to mess with.

On 25 January 1995, Manchester United were chasing their third consecutive Premier League title and faced Crystal Palace at Selhurst Park. Victory in this tricky fixture would have moved them to the top of the table. A close first half gave little indication of the drama that was to follow.

RICHARD SHAW HAD MARKED CANTONA TIGHTLY IN THE FIRST HALF AND WHEN THE TWO OF THEM TANGLED SHORTLY AFTER THE RESTART, A FRUSTRATED CANTONA KICKED OUT AT THE PALACE DEFENDER AND WAS SHOWN THE RED CARD.

Je suis Eric.

IN THE STANDS, PALACE FAN MATTHEW SIMMONS RAN DOWN THE AISLE FROM HIS SEAT IN THE 11TH ROW TO OFFER HIS OPINION. AND HERE'S WHERE THINGS GET COMPLICATED. SIMMONS LATER CLAIMED THAT HE'D SHOUTED:

Off you go, Cantona. It's an early shower for you.

WHEREAS WITNESSES ALLEGED HE SAID:

FUCK OFF BACK TO FRANCE YOU FRENCH BASTARD!!

A SUBTLE BUT CRUCIAL DIFFERENCE.

AS HE WALKED TOWARDS THE TUNNEL, CANTONA SUDDENLY TURNED AND LAUNCHED A FLYING KICK AT THE FOUL-MOUTHED MAN IN AN UGLY COAT.

NO, NOT THAT ONE.

THIS ONE:

RIB TICKLER!

HE WAS ARRESTED AND SPENT THE NIGHT RUMINATING IN A CELL.

Every moon is atrocious and every sun bitter. The ref was hard, the supporter like Hitler

THE REACTION WAS SWIFT. AMONG CANTONA'S DETRACTORS WAS THE FA'S CHIEF EXECUTIVE GRAHAM KELLY, WHO DESCRIBED THE INCIDENT AS...

A stain on the game.

HE'D OVERSEEN THE MOST HORRIFIC PERIOD IN ENGLISH FOOTBALL HISTORY, SO WAS WELL-ACQUAINTED WITH THE HUMILIATION OF FOOTBALL FANS.

MEANWHILE, ALEX FERGUSON HAD HIS OWN THEORIES ABOUT WHO WAS TO BLAME FOR THE INCIDENT...

If you'd done your fucking job, none of this would have happened.

CANTONA WAS BANNED FROM PLAYING FOR EIGHT MONTHS. HE WAS ALSO FOUND GUILTY OF COMMON ASSAULT AND SENTENCED TO COMPLETE 120 HOURS OF COMMUNITY SERVICE.

Better to die on one's feet than to live on one's knees - thirty three!

THANKFULLY, HE SPENT THE TIME COACHING KIDS, RATHER THAN CALLING BINGO. SIMMONS MEANWHILE WAS FOUND GUILTY OF USING THREATENING BEHAVIOUR AND ATTACKED A LAWYER DURING THE TRIAL.

When the solicitor follows the trawler, it is because he needs a fist in his stupid posh gob!

FREE FOR ALL
THE BOSMAN RULING

Jean-Marc Bosman wasn't a famous or decorated footballer; the high point of his career had been captaining the Belgian youth side. However, he had the enviable talent of being good enough to make a living as a professional player.

When his contract with RFC Liège came to an end in 1990, he was surprised to see that the club had offered him a new contract on a quarter of his salary. Understandably, Bosman decided it was time to move on. French club Dunkerque were keen on signing him but were unable to afford the asking price, Liège having valued Bosman at four times the amount for which they'd signed him.

Bosman took his case to the European Court of Justice. He argued that he should not be treated any differently from other employees in the European Union, just because his job involved taking throw-ins. The court agreed and ruled that players should be able to move freely once their contracts had expired. Restrictions on the number of EU players clubs could sign were also lifted.

UEFA had no choice but to apply the 'Bosman Ruling' to its forty-nine member countries, with FIFA applying the rule across all federations. Bosman's name became part of football's language but he struggled to get by as a player, having dedicated years of his life to the court case. He drifted out of football, missing out on the riches his actions created for some of his fellow professionals.

THE BOSMAN RULING IMMEDIATELY PLUNGED FOOTBALL INTO A CONDITION OF WILD PANIC, WITH VARIOUS PREDICTIONS OF THE DEATH OF CLUB FOOTBALL, PARTICULARLY IN BRITAIN.

The European Union will kill us all with its ideological assault on unfair working conditions!

I don't know what to think until I've heard the opinion of our greatest political mind.

A tsunami of migrant footballers will flood our shores!

THE GLOOM WAS LARGELY MISPLACED, BUT THE RULING GAVE MORE POWER TO PLAYERS AND HELPED ENABLE THE RISE OF THE SUPER AGENT.

CHAIRMAN

My client will also need your clothes and your motorcycle.

WAGES ROSE AS CLUBS ATTEMPTED TO RETAIN THEIR TALENT, BUT AT THE TOP LEVEL, CLUBS WERE ABLE TO OFFSET THESE EXPENSES.

GENERIC FOOTBALL CLUB

Wow! Another obscenely large TV deal. We can afford to keep our striker now!

Yeah, or we could just grossly inflate our ticket prices.

PLAYERS WERE NOW FREE TO MOVE ONCE THEIR CONTRACTS EXPIRED. THE MOST FAMOUS 'BOSMAN' DEAL IN ENGLAND SAW SPURS' CAPTAIN SOL CAMPBELL JOIN ARSENAL.

JUDAS SCUM

They may hate me now, but they will love me again when I become a politician.

THE RULING ALSO LIFTED RESTRICTIONS ON THE NUMBER OF FOREIGN PLAYERS TEAMS COULD FIELD AND BRITISH TEAMS WERE SOON PACKED WITH EXOTIC EUROPEAN IMPORTS.

ZOLA!

RAVANELLI!

KVARME!

HOWEVER, SOME CLUBS OVERSTRETCHED THEMSELVES, GIVING PLAYERS LONG-TERM CONTRACTS ON EXTORTIONATE WAGES, WITH PREDICTABLY DISASTROUS CONSEQUENCES.

We're in real trouble here. How do you feel about taking a small pay cut, for the good of the club?

THE RAINBOW WARRIORS
FRANCE 1998

France didn't appear likely to win their own World Cup in 1998. Despite taking maximum points from a fairly straightforward group, they seemed anxious and riddled with self-doubt. They lacked a goal-scorer, in an age when teams still bothered about that sort of thing. A youthful Thierry Henry was stuck out on the wing, David Trezeguet was anonymous and Stéphane Guivarc'h was showing the kind of form that would earn him a move to Newcastle United. Zidane was brilliant but still prone to the occasional, costly, act of violence. The needless stamp he administered to a Saudi player during a 4–0 stroll earned him a red card, but it at least taught him to never again behave so irresponsibly during an important World Cup game.

As the tournament progressed, the team grew bold. A golden goal win against Paraguay in the last sixteen was followed by a penalty shoot-out victory against Italy. Two goals from Lillian Thuram saw off Croatia in the semi-final and suddenly they were into the final and a 3–0 romp against a Brazil side who played as if they had recently witnessed a colleague suffer a medical emergency.

Before the competition began, bigots like Jean-Marie Le Pen had denounced the number of non-white players in the team, calling some of them 'French citizens by convenience' and claiming (falsely) that they didn't know the words of *La Marseillaise*. France's win was a victory for not only youth development but also the possibilities of multiculturalism. If there was one opportunity missed it was that the millions of people who flooded the streets after the final whistle didn't form an orderly queue and individually deliver a Nelson Muntz-style 'Ha ha!' through Le Pen's letterbox.

THE FRENCH NATIONAL TEAM HAS A LONG AND PROUD TRADITION OF FIELDING PLAYERS OF DIVERSE CULTURAL BACKGROUNDS.

BORN IN MARRAKECH

BORN TO A FAMILY OF POLISH MIGRANTS

ITALIAN LINEAGE

JUST FONTAINE MOST GOALS SCORED AT A SINGLE WORLD CUP.

RAYMOND KOPA BALLON D'OR WINNER 1958

MICHEL PLATINI EURO '84 CAPTAIN

BUT IN THE RUN UP TO THE 1998 WORLD CUP, THE LEADER OF THE FAR RIGHT NATIONAL FRONT PARTY, JEAN-MARIE LE PEN, WAS CRITICAL OF THE MULTIRACIAL MAKE-UP OF THE FRENCH SQUAD...

Look at this list of names. There must be one man among them of pure French stock? What about Zidane?

Algerian parents.

Vieira?

Born in Senegal.

Karembeu?

New Caledonia.

Desailly?

Ghana.

Henry?

Born in France

Great!

To a family from Guadeloupe. Thuram too.

Trezeguet?

Argentinian father.

Barthez?

Spanish roots.

Lizarazu?

Basque heritage.

Djorkaeff?

Armenian. As is Boghossian.

FOR GOD'S SAKE, THERE MUST BE ONE ?!

Well, there is Guivarc'h...

Is he good?

Um...

AFTER AN ANXIOUS START, THE TEAM FOUND THEIR FEET AND THE WHOLE NATION WAS SOON BEHIND THEM. MARCEL DESAILLY DESCRIBED DRIVING THROUGH TOWNS ON THE TEAM BUS AND SEEING PEOPLE OF ALL ETHNICITIES WAVING THE TRICOLOUR.

Racism is over. No more will we face insults from politicians or larger-than-life football pundits. From now on, people of all backgrounds will live together in harmony. Vive la France!

THE MERCURIAL ZIDANE SCORED TWICE IN THE FINAL AGAINST BRAZIL. HIS FACE WAS BEAMED ON TO THE ARC DE TRIOMPHE DURING A NIGHT OF WILD CELEBRATION IN PARIS.

Shit a cockerel.

AFTER THEIR STUNNING SUCCESS, OTHER COUNTRIES SOUGHT TO REPLICATE THE FRENCH MODEL.

But how can we afford such a huge investment in youth?

What? No, I just meant blaming all of our problems on immigrants and hoping that they prove us wrong.

YEAH, THIS IS PROBABLY FINE

RONALDO COLLAPSES BEFORE THE 1998 WORLD CUP FINAL

Ronaldo – the Brazilian version – was a lightning-fast, twinkle-toed genius. The sight of his round-shouldered frame dexterously dancing and swerving through the flailing limbs of panicked defenders was a joy to behold. At the age of just twenty-one, he was already the best player in the world.

His four goals at the 1998 World Cup had propelled an otherwise ordinary Brazil team to the final. But, as the players relaxed in their hotel in the hours before that final, Ronaldo mysteriously suffered a seizure, something he had never experienced before, or since.

Luckily for the young striker, if there's anyone you need on the scene during a medical emergency it's professional footballers. His room-mate, Roberto Carlos, raised the alarm and Edmundo was the first on the scene. Defender César Sampaio was the first person to administer first aid, putting his hand into Ronaldo's mouth to stop him from swallowing his tongue.

Clearly there was no way he could play in the final. No football association would be reckless enough to allow a young man who had just suffered a traumatic and potentially life-threatening experience run around playing a hard physical game just a few hours later. Would they?

MÁRIO ZAGALLO WASN'T TOLD OF RONALDO'S SEIZURE UNTIL AFTER HE WOKE FROM AN AFTERNOON NAP; HIS ASSISTANTS AND MEDICAL STAFF DECIDING NOT TO DISTURB HIM.

That's better. Now to check on what our only chance of winning has been up to.

RONALDO WAS TAKEN TO HOSPITAL AND ZAGALLO REPLACED HIM IN THE STARTING LINE-UP WITH EDMUNDO. HOWEVER, WHEN RONALDO WAS DISCHARGED HE WAS REINSTATED TO THE TEAM, MUCH TO THE ANNOYANCE OF EDMUNDO.

For God's SAKE, Edmundo! Get away from him with that strobe light!

RONALDO PLAYED LIKE A GHOST. SOON AFTER THE 3-0 DEFEAT, SPECULATION BEGAN ABOUT WHO HAD MADE THE CALL TO PICK HIM. SOME POINTED THE FINGER AT NIKE, AN ACCUSATION THEY STRONGLY DENY.

See. He's fiiine.

AN INQUEST DID REVEAL THAT NIKE'S DEAL WITH THE NATIONAL TEAM ENTITLED THEM TO ARRANGE FIVE FRIENDLIES A YEAR AND EVEN ALLOWED THEM TO SELECT THE OPPONENTS AND PICK PLAYERS.

They want us to play in Lapland in December and they want Adriano to play up front with a CGI projection of Socrates. They think it'll help to sell some trainers in the run up to Christmas.

I'd better get fit then. Pass me those McFlurries.

It was never this complicated when Topper Sports made our kit.

Topper Sports, 1984

For our investment, we demand final say on the choice of fabric softener for the team's sweatbands! No? Ok, speak to you again soon. No? Ok.

THANKFULLY, RONALDO MADE A FULL RECOVERY AND LED BRAZIL TO VICTORY IN 2002, WHEN THE ONLY HEAD-RELATED ISSUE HE FACED WAS A DAFT HAIRCUT.

What do you think? Edmundo tells me everyone's wearing their hair like this now.

MANCHESTER UNITED WIN THE TREBLE
BARCELONA, 1999

Manchester United liked to leave it late. They clinched the Premier League title on the last day of the 1998–99 season and won a thrilling FA Cup semi-final replay against Arsenal in extra-time. Ryan Giggs collected a loose pass from Patrick Vieira before burning through their defence and hammering the ball into the roof of the net. This famous goal can be carbon-dated by the amount of body hair on display when Giggs ripped off his shirt in celebration. In the final, Newcastle United offered characteristic resistance and the Red Devils won 2–0. The real drama was to come in the Champions League final against Bayern Munich.

Like the famous Ajax, Bayern and Milan teams that had preceded them, United's team included a spine of players who had emerged through their youth team: Giggsy, Scholesy, Becksy, Butty and the Nevilleseys. Each would enjoy successful careers and one of them would enjoy the bountiful rewards that come with global fame: Ryan Giggs being given the honour of carrying Louis van Gaal's clipboard.

When the famed socialist Alex Ferguson gleefully received a knighthood in 1999, it was in recognition of his long-term achievements as a manager, but also the spectacular fashion in which his Manchester United team had won a historic treble. That photo of Paul Scholes sitting on the floor during the FA Cup final had clearly left an indelible impression on the memory of Her Majesty.

GIGGS, SCHOLES, BUTT, BECKHAM AND THE NEVILLE BROTHERS ALL CAME THROUGH UNITED'S YOUTH TEAM TO FORM THE CORE OF THE CLUB'S TREBLE-WINNING SIDE. 'THE CLASS OF 92' ALSO INCLUDED ROBBIE SAVAGE. ALAS, IT SEEMS THERE WAS NEVER A CLASS EXCURSION TO A REMOTE WILDERNESS LOCATION.

Lads? Ha ha, brilliant. Ha! Lads?

BAYERN MUNICH STOOD BETWEEN THEM AND IMMORTALITY. THE GERMAN SIDE WORE A GREY KIT BUT WERE SOMEHOW ABLE TO SEE EACH OTHER AND BASLER GAVE THEM AN EARLY LEAD WITH A FREE-KICK AFTER JUST SIX MINUTES.

Wait, there's another team in this story?

BAYERN HELD THEIR LEAD AND AS THE GAME MOVED INTO INJURY TIME IT APPEARED UNITED'S DREAM WAS OVER. BUT THEN, A BECKHAM CORNER CREATED A GOALMOUTH SCRAMBLE, WHICH ENDED WITH TEDDY SHERINGHAM TURNING THE BALL INTO THE NET.

I loathe you with every fibre of my being, but even Andrew Cole would consider shaking your hand right now.

Did someone say something?

WITH SECONDS REMAINING, UNITED FORCED ANOTHER CORNER. AGAIN, BECKHAM SWUNG IN THE CROSS, SHERINGHAM FLICKED IT ON AND OLE GUNNAR SOLSKJAER STRETCHED OUT A LEG TO LIFT THE BALL INTO THE ROOF OF THE NET.

Scheiße.

CUE PANDEMONIUM.

CAPTAIN ROY KEANE WAS FORCED TO MISS THE FINAL THROUGH SUSPENSION, BUT HE CONGRATULATED HIS TEAM-MATES GLEEFULLY IN THE UNITED DRESSING ROOM.

Look at yer. Dancing about like morons. You're getting flabby. You've achieved fock all yet.

Fock. All.

Well we clearly have, so...

What the...?

Jesper fockin Blomqvist. The worst of the lot.

THIS BEING A TIME WHEN MANY ENGLISH FOOTBALL FANS STILL ROOTED FOR BRITISH TEAMS IN EUROPE, EVERYONE WAS DELIGHTED FOR THE MAN UTD FAN IN THEIR LIFE.

MEANWHILE

Ha ha ha. Magic banter, lads. Wicked.

RELATIVES

...and I want the David May duvet set and the Wes Brown coasters and the Official MUFC ear medicine and the...

COLLEAGUES

Bradford?! Ha! You should be like me and support the Champions of Europe, mate.

COMMENTATORS

As you join us for Yeovil v Crewe, we should recall the events of That Night In Barcelona...

POLYESTER PARABLE
A SHORT HISTORY OF FOOTBALL KITS

When humanity's collective lack of action on climate change results in the seas crashing through our cities, destroying civilisations and regressing society back to a pre-industrial age, there will at least be one crumb of comfort. We will no longer have to deal with the modern crime of teams wearing their change strips for absolutely no reason. Sweet blessed relief.

Football kits are a multimillion-pound industry these days, so clubs no doubt feel the need to promote their full range of kits to potential buyers: a needless away kit here, a limited-edition tribute kit there. All of them rotated on an annual basis.

Long gone are the days when simply paying an entry fee and providing vocal encouragement were enough to mark you out as a fan. The discerning grown adult now needs to be decked out in the latest polyester advertising board in order to prove their supporter credentials. Is that last season's third top you're wearing? And yet you have the front to call yourself a fan. Laughable.

IN THE VICTORIAN ERA, TEAMS WOULD OFTEN WEAR THE COLOURS OF THE SCHOOL OR SPORTS CLUB THAT FORMED THEM. AS MORE CLUBS EMERGED, THE DIVERSITY OF KIT COLOURS GREW.

What should our colours be?

Cerise, braised heart and whatever colour best represents suppressed physical desire.

I'll put biscuit.

MOST CLUBS HAD SETTLED ON A PERMANENT CHOICE BY THE TIME OF THE FIRST WORLD WAR. THERE FOLLOWED A LONG PERIOD DURING WHICH CHANGES TO SHIRTS WERE USUALLY LIMITED TO SUBTLE MODIFICATIONS TO THE COLLARS.

A round neck?! Is that even legal?

Oh yes.

Morning.

IN THE 1970s, MANUFACTURER LOGOS AND SHIRT SPONSORSHIPS STARTED TO APPEAR.

WEST GERMAN CLUB, EINTRACHT BRAUNSCHWEIG WERE THE FIRST TO WEAR A SHIRT SPONSOR, CARRYING THE LOGO OF JÄGERMEISTER IN 1973.

THIS GARMENT MAY BE THE PEAK OF HUMAN ACHIEVEMENT.

THE FIRST BRITISH CLUBS TO HAVE SHIRT SPONSORS WERE HIBS (1977)...

... AND LIVERPOOL (1979)

Bukta

HITACHI

SOME CLUBS RESISTED THIS TREND, THOUGH. FOR EXAMPLE, YEARS LATER BARCELONA STILL ONLY WEAR THE LOGOS OF A GLOBAL SPORTS CORPORATION, QATAR'S STATE AIRLINE AND A MANUFACTURER OF WASHING MACHINES.

Truly, we are more than a club.

QATAR

POLYESTER REPLACED COTTON IN THE 1980s AND KIT DESIGNS BECAME BOLDER, CULMINATING IN THE PSYCHEDELIC ERA OF THE EARLY 90s.

Sorry guys, I ate all the mushrooms.

Daniel, don't move. You've just designed the new Norwich top.

NOWADAYS, KITS ARE SERIOUS BUSINESS, WITH ANNUAL LAUNCHES ACCOMPANIED BY MOODY PHOTOSHOOTS AND GRAND SLOGANS.

Yeah, I want to hire a dry ice machine; I've got the Crawley Town players coming in later. Also, do you do snow leopards?

ALTHOUGH THESE ARE MORE SOBER TIMES, THERE ARE STILL SOME DESIGNERS WHO EXPERIENCE THE OCCASIONAL NINETIES ACID FLASHBACK.

CULTURAL LEONESA (2014)

THE SAIPAN STROP
ROY KEANE LEAVES THE 2002 WORLD CUP

Roy Keane's nostrils flared as he surveyed the chaotic scene before him at Dublin Airport. Fans, journalists, TV crews, all clambering over scattered piles of luggage to see the Ireland team off to the 2002 World Cup. Even the Taoiseach, Bertie Ahern, was present. Keane's mood worsened when he noticed that the FAI top brass were sitting in business class while the players were cramped into economy. He silently seethed. Say nothing, Roy, keep it together. We'll soon be on the training ground, they can't hurt you there.

However, when they got to Saipan, the quality of the pitch was poor and the permanent cloud above Keane's head grew darker when he saw the condition of the training kit and dietary plans. There was a storm coming. His concerns about the ability of manager Mick McCarthy deepened and his frustration boiled over during a row about who would go in goal during a five-a-side match. He decided to quit and informed McCarthy.

Keane had a change of heart but went on to list all of his complaints in an interview with the *Irish Times*. 'What's all this?' asked a furious McCarthy, holding up a copy of the paper during a team meeting. Things escalated from there and the meeting ended with Keane instructing McCarthy to 'stick the World Cup up your arse', which was at least anatomically possible, unlike the follow-up suggestion that he 'stick it up your bollocks'. Keane was sent home and Ireland lost on penalties to Spain in the second round.

Although instilled with a unique winning mentality that enabled him to achieve so much as a player, Roy Keane may not have been the easiest of people to spend time with.

I've spoken to Sir Alex and he reckons I should stick around, but I'm **THIS** close to walking away from this caravanning holiday. **THIS** close.

The travel arrangements say it all. Leaving the motorway at junction 15 added half an hour to our journey.

And yeah, you might say, 'you were driving, Roy', but this is a team game. I can't do it all.

And on that, let's talk about the seating. I'm up the front doing all the hard work while you stretch out back here, snoozing and farting.

As for the diet, I'm astonished that you think a steak slice and a packet of Starburst are an appropriate choice for a professional athlete.

You'll probably say 'Roy, you bought them from the service station but again it's just excuses.

I saw that Muhammad Ali film, starring The Fresh Prince of Bel Air. The Fresh Prince of Bel Air didn't accept second best and he definitely wouldn't have put up with this level of disorganisation.

Teaspoons in the fork section!

CRACK

That hurt more than missing the Champions League final.

Oh, you think I'm exaggerating the seriousness of this injury?

I don't have to put up with this. You can stick your mini-break right up your bollocks.

SLAM
FLOUNCE

AGAIN 1966
SOUTH KOREA 2 ITALY 1, 2002

'Italy are out because they *will not learn*', snapped the BBC commentator Barry Davies, like an exasperated Latin teacher. He'd just seen South Korea come from behind to beat Italy with an extra-time golden goal and his admonishment of the *Azzurri*'s negativity gave British TV viewers a hearty lunchtime laugh.

In Seoul, three million people celebrated on the streets, in scenes that would have been spectacular unless you had to pop over to the all-night garage to pick up some milk.

South Korea's manager Guus Hiddink had been under pressure before the start of the tournament, but their group stage wins against Poland and Portugal, and now this result against Italy, elevated him to the status of a national hero. In the next round they beat Spain and the stadium was renamed in Hiddink's honour. He was also given honorary citizenship and free flights for life.

The mood in Italy was less cheery. Rather than focus on Giovanni Trapattoni's cautious tactics, they heaped blame upon the referee. Italy had seen four goals disallowed during the group stage and this latest officiating atrocity clearly pointed to an international conspiracy; a plot that went as deep as teaching their strikers to balloon a succession of easy chances.

AS THE TEAMS EMERGED, THE SOUTH KOREAN FANS HELD UP WHITE CARDS TO REVEAL THE MESSAGE: 'AGAIN 1966'.

What the hell, man? That was a victory for the Democratic People's Republic, not those bourgeois southern soft-bellies!

THE HOSTS WERE AWARDED A PENALTY IN THE FOURTH MINUTE, BUT BUFFON SAVED AHN'S KICK AND VIERI THEN HEADED ITALY INTO THE LEAD.

Shhh...

The best thing about that goal celebration is that it DEFINITELY WONT BACKFIRE.

GIOVANNI TRAPATTONI IMMEDIATELY INSTRUCTED HIS TEAM TO SHUT UP SHOP. AND IT LOOKED TO HAVE WORKED UNTIL A PANUCCI ERROR, TWO MINUTES FROM TIME, SET UP SEOL KI-HYEON TO LEVEL.

Even 'Il Trap' has to admit that's quite funny.

THERE FOLLOWED A SUCCESSION OF MISSED CHANCES AND QUESTIONABLE OFFICIATING, WHICH INCLUDED A RED CARD FOR TOTTI FOR DIVING IN THE BOX. REPLAYS SHOWED HE HAD CLEARLY BEEN FOULED.

Ohhhhhhh, 'AGAIN 1966'. I get it now: refereeing decisions that heavily favour the home team. Put the missiles back in the storage facility; it's all sweet.

Naw

STILL, THIS COULD ALL HAVE BEEN ACADEMIC HAD VIERI NOT SKIED A SIMPLE CHANCE FROM SIX YARDS OUT.

THEN, IN THE DYING MINUTES OF EXTRA-TIME, AHN JUNG-HWAN ROSE ABOVE MALDINI TO HEAD IN A GOLDEN GOAL TO WIN THE TIE...

Uh-oh.

AND IMMEDIATELY HAD HIS CONTRACT WITH SERIE A CLUB PERUGIA CANCELLED.

PERUGIA'S OWNER LUCIANO GAUCCI LATER RELENTED, BUT AHN STEERED CLEAR ANYWAY. A CONTROVERSIAL FIGURE, GAUCCI LATER SIGNED COLONEL GADAFFI'S SON AND THREATENED TO FIELD A HORSE IN A MATCH.

Warm up, Daisy, I've made a massive mistake.

ITALY'S REAL FURY WAS RESERVED FOR REFEREE BYRON MORENO, AND IF THERE WAS ONE THING ITALIAN FOOTBALL KNEW ABOUT, IT WAS DODGY REFEREES.

LUCIANO MOGGI, JUVENTUS

Who the hell is this fool?! We didn't select him, has he even been briefed on what to do?

THEY MIGHT HAVE BEEN ON TO SOMETHING, THOUGH. IN 2010, HE WAS ARRESTED IN NEW YORK WHILE TRYING TO SMUGGLE SEVERAL KILOGRAMS OF HEROIN INTO THE U.S.

Shhh...

ROMAN'S EMPIRE
ABRAMOVICH BUYS CHELSEA

In 2003, the idea of a billionaire from overseas buying a British football club was a novelty. Before Roman Abramovich bought Chelsea, supporters would pin their hopes on a local sugar daddy coming to their rescue. Within six weeks of taking charge, Abramovich had spent £140 million on new players. The game had been changed.

Abramovich acquired his fortune through the privatisation of the Russian oil industry. He and the other oligarchs negotiated a cut-price deal with President Yeltsin and the consequent sale of that oil had made Abramovich the second richest person in Russia. The purchase of a highly visible asset such as Chelsea would reduce the risk of Yeltsin's successor, Vladimir Putin, trying to reclaim some of that fortune. Thankfully, any moral objections to his takeover of Chelsea are redundant because: football.

Before his arrival, Chelsea had debts of £80 million. Everyone was delighted that he had chosen to buy them, of all clubs. He could have picked anyone; *anyone but them.*

Chelsea went on to become one of the most successful clubs in England, expanding their popularity across the world. Abramovich remains a mysterious character, his blankly grinning face is occasionally seen at matches, looking down from a seat in the executive suite. To mock such a powerful man in a cartoon book probably shows the kind of bravery that should be rewarded by some sort of reward. A financial reward. Just to clarify.

IT'S 2003 AND THE RUSSIAN OLIGARCH, ROMAN ABRAMOVICH, IS IN THE MARKET FOR A HIGH-PROFILE BUSINESS. WE JOIN HIM AS HE SCOURS BRITAIN IN HIS PRIVATE AIRBORNE YACHT.

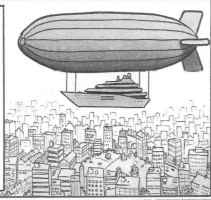

How about that one?

That's Griffin Park, sir.

What is it, a sewage treatment plant? Do the people think fondly of it?

Sort of and sort of.

How about that one with the superfluous hotel complex and grotesque animatronic gnome?

Right, we need to electrify that fence to divert the punters past the half and half scarf stalls.

Whatever. Lose the goblin though.

AND SO ROMAN BECAME THE NEW OWNER OF CHELSEA, WHICH CLEARLY PRESENTED THEIR FANS WITH A COMPLEX MORAL DILEMMA.

We've signed Damien Duff!

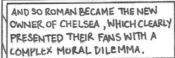

MEANWHILE, ROMAN SETTLED BACK AND BEGAN TO ENJOY A NEW HOBBY THAT WOULD BRING HIM IMMENSE PERSONAL PLEASURE.

GREEK LIGHTNING
GREECE WIN EURO 2004

Greece had never won a match at a major tournament and that wasn't a statistic that was likely to change at the 2004 European Championship. Despite being coached by the respected German, Otto Rehhagel, they were still 80-1 outsiders. Expectations were further diminished by the state of the domestic game in Greece. The top clubs had amassed huge debts and attendances had plummeted in the face of increasing spectator violence. At least a short trip to Portugal would provide a brief distraction.

You won't believe what happened next.

Three weeks later their captain (and player of the tournament), Theo Zagorakis, was lifting the trophy after a 1–0 win against Portugal. They'd previously seen off Spain, Russia, France and the Czech Republic. Behind Zagorakis, 15,000 Greek fans roared as much in astonishment as delight. King Otto had conquered Europe and this would surely signal the beginning of a prosperous new era for Greece. You won't believe...etc.

NOTE TO THE READER

THE TEMPTATION WHEN REFLECTING UPON GREECE'S SHOCK WIN AT EURO 2004 IS TO EMPLOY IMAGERY FROM GREEK MYTHOLOGY. THIS WELL-WORN CLICHÉ DOES A DISSERVICE TO THE MODERN, VIBRANT GREECE AND THE EFFORTS OF ITS FOOTBALLERS. IT IS THE LAZY WRITER WHO RELIES UPON SUCH HACKNEYED TROPES. HERE GOES THEN...

Kneel before Otto, God of Pragmatism. Flood the midfield. Maximise your set pieces.

SEVEN NEW STADIUMS WERE BUILT IN PORTUGAL FOR THE FINALS AND SOME OF THEM ARE STILL IN USE TODAY! VISITING GREEK DIGNITARIES WERE IMPRESSED.

Seeing all these new stadiums makes me feel certain that we've done the right thing in massively over-spending on Olympic venues.

Either way, now we're in the Eurozone, all our problems are over.

THE OPENING CEREMONY CELEBRATED PORTUGAL'S PROUD NAVAL HISTORY. GREECE STUNNED THEIR HOSTS WITH A 2-1 WIN, AFTER WHICH THEY WERE DUBBED 'THE PIRATE SHIP'.

Sounds about right.

Oh calm down, Angela, you'll almost probably get your money back.

IT DIDN'T MATTER THAT THEIR FORWARD LINE WAS LESS MOBILE THAN THE ELGIN MARBLES BECAUSE THEIR GERMAN COACH, OTTO REHHAGEL, HAD A SIMPLE BUT EFFECTIVE GAME PLAN...

1. DEFEND SO DEEPLY THAT YOU DISCOVER THE LOST CITY OF ATLANTIS.

2. HIT THE OPPOSITION WITH A CLINICAL, SURPRISE ATTACK.

Everyone into the Trojan Jan Koller. The Czechs won't suspect a thing.

GREECE'S DEFEAT OF PORTUGAL IN THE FINAL WAS A SHOCK GREATER THAN THE ONE EXPERIENCED BY UNSEASONED TRAVELLERS UPON THEIR FIRST VISIT TO A GREEK BATHROOM.

Don't bother unpacking, babe. We're leaving.

Eh?

THEIR WIN GAVE HOPE TO EVERY NATION THAT HAS FOUND SUCCESS ELUSIVE. THEY NOW SAW THAT WITH A DECENT MANAGER, A STRONG PLAN AND DISCIPLINED PLAYERS, ANYONE COULD 'DO A GREECE'.

Anyone?

YEAH, NOT YOU, MATE.

THE INVINCIBLES
ARSENAL'S 2003-04 SEASON

Arsène Wenger was virtually unknown in England before his arrival at Arsenal in 1996, this being an age before both the internet and hipsters. Wenger had glasses, a foreign accent and knew about things like stretching and not drinking eight pints of Stella the night before a game. English football at the time was renowned for its willingness to embrace intelligence (players with two O levels were often nicknamed 'Professor', such was the reverence for education) and so he was welcomed warmly.

Arsenal won the double in his second season and repeated the feat in 2002, going the whole season without losing an away league game. Wenger's claims that his team could beat this and remain undefeated throughout the entire 2003–04 season raised eyebrows. After all, no team had achieved this since Preston North End in 1888-89.

However, Wenger was wise (glasses, accent) and his pronouncement came true. Arsenal would not lose a league game between May 2003 and October 2005, earning them a Premier League title and the moniker The Invincibles. Arsenal supporters would never forget this astonishing achievement and Wenger earned their lifelong respect.

ARSENAL FC

THE **INVINCIBLES**

2003/04 SEASON

JENS LEHMANN

THE RANTY PERSON WHOSE EYES YOU AVOID ON PUBLIC TRANSPORT

ARSÈNE WENGER

INVENTED PASTA

LAUREN

NO NONSENSE

KOLO TOURÉ

SOME NONSENSE

SOL CAMPBELL

MAN OF THE PEOPLE

ASHLEY COLE

'MR ARSENAL'

FREDDIE LJUNGBERG

UNDERWEAR MODEL

GILBERTO SILVA

My friend, nothing would give me greater pleasure than helping you to delouse your dog.

GOOD BLOKE

PATRICK VIEIRA

TELESCOPIC LEGS

ROBERT PIRÈS

SMASHING THE OPPOSITION'S SYSTEM

MARTIN KEOWN

MIND-ALTERING SUPER POWERS

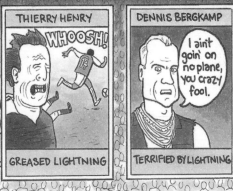

THIERRY HENRY

WHOOSH!

GREASED LIGHTNING

DENNIS BERGKAMP

I ain't goin' on no plane, you crazy fool.

TERRIFIED BY LIGHTNING

SUPPORTING CAST

EDU, PARLOUR, ALIADIÈRE, CYGAN, REYES, WILTORD, CLICHY, KANU, PAT RICE

THE DUDEK FINAL
LIVERPOOL WIN THE 2005 CHAMPIONS LEAGUE

Carlo Ancelotti predicted that his Milan team would score within the first three minutes. As it turned out they did it within one. Liverpool's defence was barely out of their tracksuit tops by the time Maldini volleyed in a Pirlo free-kick. By half-time the lead had been extended to three and Liverpool were facing certain defeat.

However, in reaching the final the Reds had already shown a tenacious fighting spirit, including a stunning semi-final win against Chelsea that Real Madrid's sporting director Jorge Valdano likened to 'a shit hanging from a stick'. Milan were about to receive a taste of that stick.

When Steven Gerrard's low forehead connected with a John Arne Riise cross in the fifty-fourth minute, the comeback was on. Within six minutes they were level. First, Vladimír Šmicer hit an angled shot that skidded across the turf to beat Dida. Then Gerrard went over a Gattuso challenge in the area. There could be no doubt it was a penalty, as Gerrard had previously said that it was mostly foreign players who dive. Alonso's spot kick was saved but he raced in to scoop the rebound into the net.

In the Liverpool goal Jerzy Dudek was enjoying the game of his life. A breathtaking double save from Shevchenko in extra-time meant the final would be decided on penalties. Dudek was again the hero in the shoot-out, saving the spot kicks of Pirlo and Shevchenko to help Liverpool to lift the cup. Pirlo would later liken the memory of this final to a lodged suppository – 'Every now and then I feel it move, letting me know that it's still there, asserting its presence. It calls me by name and it's a pain in the arse in the truest sense of the term.' Perhaps a stick would have come in handy.

THE GREATEST MOMENT IN THE HISTORY OF SPORT
BURY'S CHRIS BRASS SCORES AN OWN GOAL WITH HIS FACE

When: 22 April 2006

Where: the Williamson Motors Stadium, Darlington

Who: Chris Brass

What: a League Two encounter between Darlington and Bury. Attempting an overhead clearance, Bury's Brass volleys the ball directly into his own face, almost breaking his nose in the process. The ball flies into his own net, past a stunned goalkeeper. It becomes the defining image of the decade and some consider it to be the day that Darlington lost its innocence.

Why: because football is a beautiful, cruel, hilarious mystery.

AS FOOTAGE OF BRASS'S OWN GOAL SPREAD THROUGHOUT BRITAIN VIA BLOCKY YOUTUBE VIDEOS AND LATE-NIGHT FOOTBALL LEAGUE HIGHLIGHTS SHOWS...

... SOCIETY BEGAN TO CRUMBLE. IF PEOPLE COULD JUST VOLLEY FOOTBALLS INTO THEIR OWN FACES THEN WHERE DID THE BOUNDARIES LIE? ANARCHY RULED.

THE NATION'S INFRASTRUCTURE SOON COLLAPSED, ALTHOUGH THERE WAS NO DISCERNABLE DIFFERENCE TO SERVICE QUALITY.

I've been waiting for this train to arrive for six days, which is about the level of efficiency I have come to expect.

CHAOS REIGNED IN THE FINANCIAL SECTOR TOO, CRIPPLING THE ECONOMY...

The market is anxious! It's as if it were a living, sentient being, rather than just an office tower full of coke-addled sociopaths shouting at each other.

IN AN ATTEMPT TO RESTORE ORDER, PRIME MINISTER TONY BLAIR ADDRESSED THE PEOPLE

My record as Prime Minister has been typified by honesty and integrity. The British people should therefore trust me when I say that our government has this situation under control.

How bad is the situation really?

I understand that the video's central protagonist has Paul Weller hair, sir.

It's worse than I feared. Ready my escape pod.

But sir, it hasn't been tested...

God damn it, do I strike you as the kind of man who waits for 'evidence' before ploughing headlong into a potentially disastrous mission?!

This was entirely justifiiii iiiiiiiiiii iiiiiiiiied!

GOING OUT WITH A BANG
ZIDANE'S HEAD-BUTT

Like many of the great artists, Zinedine Zidane was ingrained with a self-destructive streak. They all had it: Vincent van Gogh, Lenny Bruce, Kurt Cobain, Screech from *Saved by the Bell*. It was as if the weight of creating beauty had to be balanced with havoc. One minute Zidane would be pirouetting through midfield with delicate grace (for a big man), the next he'd be using his studs to peel the flesh off a full-back's shinbone.

A case in point was the 2006 World Cup final – Zidane's last match as a professional. His performances had carried the French through, with assists and goals helping to see off Spain, Brazil and Portugal. In the final they would face Italy. Only seven minutes had passed before a Zidane penalty had given France the lead, the perfect end to an august career. Sure, he'd opted to chip the kick against the underside of the bar and the ball had only crossed the line by the width of one of the wispy hairs on his balding head, but everything was definitely going to be all right.

ARGUABLY FRANCE'S GREATEST EVER PLAYER, ZIDANE WAS CONVINCED TO COME OUT OF INTERNATIONAL RETIREMENT AFTER A 3AM TALK WITH AN UN-NAMED PERSON.

If I agree, will you let me go back to sleep?

Yeeees...

HIS PERFORMANCES INSPIRED 'LES BLEUS' TO THE FINAL AND HE GAVE THEM THE LEAD FROM THE PENALTY SPOT AFTER MARCO MATERAZZI'S CLUMSY FOUL ON MALOUDA – A PLAYER WHO HAD MISSED THE START OF THE TOURNAMENT DUE TO HAEMORRHOIDS

THIS IS NO LONGER FUNNY ONCE YOU HIT MIDDLE AGE.

BELIEVE ME.

MATERAZZI HIMSELF EQUALISED AND THE GAME WENT INTO EXTRA-TIME. ELEVEN MINUTES FROM THE END, AS THE BALL WAS CLEARED FROM THE ITALIAN BOX, MATERAZZI COULD BE SEEN ANTAGONISING ZIDANE. WHAT WAS SAID REMAINS A MYSTERY, BUT WHATEVER IT WAS, IT HAD THE DESIRED EFFECT.

Something rude about your family and/or cultural heritage.

Camus was a deeply inferior goalkeeper.

Sure, French wine is fine, if you like that sort of thing, but if you want real quality, go Italian.

Player one activates rutting stag mode!

What have I done to deserve this?

IN THE ITV COMMENTARY BOX, CLIVE TYLDESLEY SPECULATES WHETHER MATERAZZI HAD TWEAKED ZIDANE'S NIPPLE. THE MENTAL IMAGE OF THE WORD ROLLING OFF TYLDESLEY'S TONGUE ENDURES.

Nipple

Nipple

Nipple

CHRIST.

DID HE DELIBERATELY END HIS CAREER ON SUCH A DESTRUCTIVE NOTE BECAUSE HE WAS UNCOMFORTABLE WITH ADULATION AND ATTENTION? THIS THEORY WOULD BE MORE CREDIBLE IF HE'D CHOSEN TO SPEND HIS RETIREMENT SANDING DOWN OLD BOATS, RATHER THAN MANAGING REAL MADRID.

How did he even get it in here?

RONALDO 7

BALE

AN UNQUESTIONING WELCOME
SHEIKH MANSOUR BUYS
MANCHESTER CITY

Manchester City supporters reacted with caution when news emerged that Sheikh Mansour, a member of the ruling family of Abu Dhabi, was buying their club. The United Arab Emirates was an undemocratic nation with a troublesome human rights record to say the least. City fans expressed this wariness through the wholesale purchase of Arabian headwear and the creation of banners welcoming their new Emirati overlords. After all, there were rumours they were going to sign Wayne Bridge.

By this point City fans probably felt they hadn't had much luck with owners. They protested for years for the removal of Peter Swales and were thrilled when he was deposed by Franny Lee, a former terrace hero turned successful entrepreneur who had made a fortune from the toilet paper industry. He arrived with a range of ambitious statements that, much like his business interests, turned out to be based in shite.

The club were later owned by Thaksin Shinawatra, the former Prime Minister of Thailand, who oversaw the deaths of 2,500 people during his government's 'war on drugs'. The notoriously reticent City fans nicknamed him Frank and showered him with affection. Well, he *did* know the words to 'Blue Moon'.

However, the new owners were able to bring the success that City had so long craved. Eventually they would extend their reach beyond just Manchester City, creating the City Football Group, which owns a network of clubs around the world.

"What's all this?"

"Paul, these men are from the City Football Group"

"Allow me to explain. The City Football Group has identified that there remain some pockets of ideological resistance to our quest for global market domination..."

"We therefore intend to purchase each individual household and turn the entire population into powerful advocates for our brand."

"But I'm a Charlton fan."

"Not any more, Paul. They've offered to buy us a new sofa and sort out the decking in the garden. All we need to do is aggressively market their preferred airline to our friends and family and change the kids' names to a hashtag of their choosing."

"OK, that all sounds fine, but who are they...?"

"Scott Sinclair and Richard Wright. We've taken them on loan for a year. They're going to help out around the house and entertain the kids."

"This is a great opportunity to get some game time under our belts and we can't wait to get cracking on that decking SOMEONE said they'd put down two summers ago."

"Ahem... heh ...yes."

THE WAR TO END ALL WARS
MESSI v RONALDO

The early part of the twenty-first century has been characterised by a bitter conflict between two ideologically opposed belief systems: People Who Like Leo versus People Who Like Ronnie. Everyone has been forced to pick a side in the ongoing war of attrition between two footballers who actually seem to get on perfectly well.

Arguments often centre on the pair's differing personalities. Messi is usually painted as a saintly paragon of virtue, cruelly persecuted by the Spanish tax authorities; Ronaldo as a preening cry baby.

Their fame transcends football, stretching into all areas of life. For example, prior to giving a speech at the Conservative Party Conference in 2015, George Osborne and Theresa May imitated Ronaldo's famous manspreading free-kick stance. Presumably, Osborne had caught a glimpse of Ronaldo lining up a shot and assumed that was the way that all humans stood, like that bit in *Splash* when Daryl Hannah learns to speak English from watching television.

AS FOOTBALL HAS MOVED MORE DEEPLY INTO THE WORLD OF SHOWBIZ AND CELEBRITY, A CURIOUS NEW BREED OF FAN HAS EMERGED: PEOPLE WHO SUPPORT INDIVIDUAL PLAYERS RATHER THAN CLUBS.

What team do you support?

Nicolás Otamendi

FOR SOME, WATCHING TELEVISED COVERAGE OF AN AWARDS CEREMONY IS MORE SATISFYING THAN ATTENDING AN ACTUAL MATCH.

LIVE HD

THIS PHENOMENON HAS ARGUABLY COME ABOUT AS A RESULT OF THE ESCALATING RIVALRY BETWEEN THE GLOBAL MEGASTARS OF...

LIONEL MESSI

AND CRISTIANO RONALDO

RONALDO

Hey, if I sit like that on public transport, everyone will respect me!

THE PAIR HAVE TERRORISED DEFENCES IN LA LIGA AND EUROPE FOR THE LAST DECADE AS THEY BATTLE TO ESTABLISH OUTRIGHT SUPREMACY.

Phew, another hat-trick and another record broken. Nobody can catch me—

Um, Leo, Ronaldo's just scored a million goals against Getafe.

AS WELL AS WINNING LEAGUE TITLES AND CHAMPIONS LEAGUE MEDALS, THEIR MASTERY HAS BEEN RECOGNISED THROUGH LONG-TERM DOMINANCE OF THE BALLON D'OR.

All eyes will be on Ronnie tonight. No one will upstage me. Now for a quick spray of Lynx Java and—

Come quick! Messi has come dressed like Artie Ziff from The Simpsons and it's spectacular!

THE ONE-UPMANSHIP HAS EVEN SEEN RONALDO HAVE A DISTANT GALAXY NAMED IN HIS HONOUR.

OTAMENDI

IT REMAINS TO BE SEEN HOW MESSI WILL RESPOND, BUT IN THE MEANTIME THE WORLD CAN BUSY ITSELF ARGUING OVER WHO IS TRULY THE GREATEST PLAYER OF THIS GENERATION.

It is Zlatan.

Do not look at Zlatan.

THE FRENCH REVOLUTION
FRANCE IMPLODE AT THE
2010 WORLD CUP

France's qualification for the 2010 World Cup was controversial. During a play-off against Ireland, Thierry Henry controlled the ball with his hand before passing to William Gallas, who headed in the winning goal. The Football Association of Ireland complained at length, but their chief executive John Delaney later claimed that FIFA had paid the FAI off to drop their case.

Before France even arrived in South Africa there were rumours of conflict between playmaker Yoann Gourcuff and the more experienced members of the squad, namely Franck Ribéry and Thierry Henry. Henry had been told he wouldn't be part of the starting line-up at the World Cup and the perception in France was that he spent the tournament pouting.

They started dreadfully. A goalless draw with Uruguay was followed by a 2–0 loss to Mexico, during which Nicolas Anelka was substituted at half-time. He confronted coach Raymond Domenech, allegedly saying 'go get fucked up the arse, you dirty son of a whore', which probably sounds more romantic in French. He refused to apologise and was packed off home.

Inexplicably, things would then get even worse. During a public training session, Patrice Evra had a huge argument with the fitness coach, Robert Duverne. The players stropped off to the team bus, drew the curtains and refused to come back. Evra then issued Domenech with a statement from the squad, detailing their anger at not being consulted over Anelka's punishment.

Unsurprisingly, they limped to a 2–1 defeat in their final game, against South Africa, and were knocked out. Caustic to the end, they did just enough to prevent the hosts from progressing, too.

In the aftermath, Jean-Pierre Escalettes resigned as president of the French Football Federation and was soon joined by Domenech, whose famed use of astrology had failed to predict what a colossal disaster the whole occasion would be.

STAR CHART BOLLOCKS

WITH

RAYMOND

DOMENECH

ARIES — FRANCK RIBÉRY

THAT LITTLE PRICK GOURCUFF IS ALWAYS GIVING YOU EVILS. TRY WORKING WITH OTHERS TO UNDERMINE HIM. IT'S A TEAM SPORT.

TAURUS — PATRICE EVRA

THE FRENCH PEOPLE LOVE A REVOLUTIONARY. LEAD A PLAYER REBELLION MID-TOURNAMENT. SEE HOW THAT WORKS OUT FOR YOU.

CANCER — YOANN GOURCUFF

CHALLENGES WITH THE ELDER GENERATION WILL TYPIFY YOUR WEEK. BE PERSISTENT AND YOU'LL REAP THE REWARDS.

GEMINI — JEAN-PIERRE ESCALETTES

SORTIE

YOU DON'T NEED THIS SHIT.

LEO — THIERRY HENRY

EVERYONE LIKES A SULKER AND ON YOUR DAY YOU'RE ONE OF THE BEST. A BLANKET ACROSS THE KNEES WILL GARNER MASS PUBLIC SYMPATHY.

VIRGO — FRENCH JOURNALIST

I FORESEE YOU PENNING A SYMPATHETIC STORY ON A DEVILISHLY HANDSOME FOOTBALL MANAGER DOING HIS BEST IN DIFFICULT CIRCUMSTANCES.

LIBRA — JOHN DELANEY

YOU MAY HAVE COME INTO AN UNEXPECTED WINDFALL RECENTLY. THE LADS IN THE MEDIA WILL LOVE YOUR CHUTZPAH. MILK IT, YOU'VE DESERVED IT.

SCORPIO — FRENCH FOOTBALL FEDERATION PR MANAGER

YEAH, YOU SHOULD PROBABLY JUST THROW YOUR PHONE INTO A WATERFALL.

SAGITTARIUS — KARIM BENZEMA

YOU MAY HAVE MISSED OUT ON A WORK TRIP, BUT USE THE TIME TO REFLECT UPON HOW PROFESSIONALLY YOU'LL CONDUCT YOURSELF WHEN YOU GET YOUR CHANCE.

CAPRICORN — FRANCE TEAM BUS DRIVER

SOME OVERTIME COULD BE ON THE CARDS THIS WEEK. EASIEST MONEY YOU'LL EVER MAKE. YOU WON'T EVEN NEED TO DO MUCH DRIVING.

PISCES — NICOLAS ANELKA

I SEE A LONG, SURPRISE JOURNEY IN YOUR FUTURE. YOUR SUNNY DISPOSITION WILL HELP YOU THROUGH.

AQUARIUS — RAYMOND DOMENECH

YOU'RE DOING AN AWESOME JOB, KEEP UP THE GOOD WORK! AVOID NEWSPAPERS THIS WEEK. PROBABLY BEST TO STAY AWAY FROM TV AND THE INTERNET TOO.

THE INVENTION OF PASSING
TIKA TAKA

There used to be a comforting reliability about Spain. At every major tournament they would arrive with a great squad of players, promising to put aside the animosity of the domestic season and make amends for their underachieving past. This would be their year. Their consequent capitulation became as much a part of the traditional World Cup routine as the release of the sticker collection or booing Sepp Blatter.

This all began to change in the late 2000s with the arrival of a tactical system that involved pressing opponents when not in possession and then keeping hold of the ball until the other team loses the will to live. This system would come to be known as 'Tika Taka' – reflecting the sound made by the billion short passes tapped around the Spanish midfield before they debase themselves by having a shot. It would enable Spain to win a World Cup and two European Championships and robbed us all of the chance to enjoy them failing to negotiate a group containing Paraguay, Bulgaria and Nigeria.

Thankfully, the last couple of tournaments have seen a return to normalcy, with early Spanish exits reminding us of simpler times.

UNSURPRISINGLY, IT WAS THE VISIONARY JOHAN CRUYFF WHO WAS INSTRUMENTAL IN ESTABLISHING BARCELONA'S YOUTH ACADEMY AT 'LA MASIA', AN 18TH CENTURY CATALAN FARMHOUSE.

I want a production line of telepathic uber children who can rise to dominate World football.

LA MASIA PRODUCED MANY GIFTED FOOTBALLERS, BUT IT WAS THE CROP OF PLAYERS WHO FORMED THE SPINE OF PEP GUARDIOLA'S TEAM OF 2008-2012 THAT MADE THE BIGGEST IMPACT.

THE SPANISH NATIONAL TEAM FINALLY REALISED ITS POTENTIAL TOO, BY ADOPTING THE SAME CORE PRINCIPLES OF PASSING, PRESSING AND NOT HAVING A MASSIVE ROW WITHIN MINUTES OF ARRIVING AT THE TRAINING CAMP.

PRE-TIKA-TAKA

I can't wait for us to get knocked out so I don't have to look at your stupid Catalan face.

I spat in your eggs.

SIX LA MASIA ALUMNI WERE IN SPAIN'S STARTING LINE-UP THAT WON THE 2010 WORLD CUP FINAL. DURING THE MATCH, THE NETHERLANDS' NIGEL DE JONG DID HIT UPON ONE WAY TO INTERRUPT THE PROCESSION OF PASSING.

Total football!

HOWEVER, SPAIN WERE GENERALLY UNSTOPPABLE, RETAINING THE EUROPEAN CHAMPIONSHIP IN 2012. A SCHISM EMERGED BETWEEN THOSE WHO LOVED THEIR STYLE OF PLAY AND THOSE WHO FOUND THEIR DOMINANCE DULL.

Truly we are blessed to be alive at a time to witness the miracle of Xavi and Iniesta exchanging sideways passes for 90 minutes.

This is like the pipe screensaver, but the pipes never change colour and Michael Owen is providing analysis of the pipes.

THIS BATTLE WAS MOSTLY PLAYED OUT ONLINE AND CREATED A LONG-LASTING BITTERNESS THAT COULD PREVENT PEOPLE WHO POST ON INTERNET FORUMS FROM EVER WINNING THE WORLD CUP.

GUARDIOLA LEFT BARCELONA IN 2012, BUT THE TIKA-TAKA PHILOSOPHY LIVES ON, WITH SUCCESSIVE MANAGERS EXPLORING EXCITING NEW AVENUES. LUIS ENRIQUE WORE A SUIT WITH TRAINERS AND NO SOCKS TO THE 2015 CHAMPIONS LEAGUE FINAL, FOR EXAMPLE.

Més Que Un Boat Shoe

AND THEIR PLAYERS CONTINUE TO DISPLAY TECHNICAL BRILLIANCE, EVEN MASTERING THE SKILL OF INVISIBILITY. AT THIS STAGE, LUIS SUÁREZ COULD MURDER AN OPPONENT AND NOT GET SENT OFF.

Well this is a genuine mystery.

QATAR

'AGÜEROOOOOOOO!'
MANCHESTER CITY WIN THE PREMIER LEAGUE

Manchester City and Manchester United went into the last day of the 2011–12 season level on points at the top of the Premier League, separated only by City's superior goal difference. Despite the massive cash investment from their wealthy new owners, the title had thus far eluded City. They knew that a home win against lowly QPR would be enough to bring them their first league title since the 1960s, but this was Manchester City so calamity couldn't be ruled out. United would need to record an enormous win to overhaul City, but they were playing Sunderland so it wasn't entirely unthinkable either.

The City players emerged from the tunnel to a golden shower of tickertape, the cameras cutting away to Liam Gallagher holding aloft a scarf emblazoned with 'Champions 2012'. They weren't so much tempting fate as sending it filthy selfies via direct message.

What followed was the most dramatic conclusion to a season since football began, some twenty years earlier.

MANCHESTER UNITED ARRIVED AT SUNDERLAND KNOWING THAT THEY HAD TO WIN AND HOPE THAT CITY SLIPPED UP. HOWEVER, THE STADIUM OF LIGHT WAS NEVER AN EASY PLACE TO VISIT FOR FERGUSON'S MEN.

If one of my players trips on that red carpet, there'll be hell to pay, laddie.

Yes, Sir Alex.

UNITED AND CITY BOTH HELD NARROW 1-0 LEADS AT HALF-TIME, BUT THE REAL DRAMA WAS YET TO COME.

SHORTLY AFTER THE RESTART, A MIS-DIRECTED HEADER FROM CITY'S JOLEON LESCOTT SET UP CISÉ TO LEVEL FOR QPR

AFTER AN HOUR, QPR'S MORRISSEY-AND-PHILOSOPHER-QUOTING MIDFIELDER, JOEY BARTON, REALISED HE WASN'T THE CENTRE OF THE STORY SO ELBOWED CARLOS TEVEZ IN THE THROAT. AFTER BEING SHOWN THE RED CARD, HE THEN KICKED SERGIO AGÜERO AND TRIED TO START A FIGHT WITH THE CITY SUBSTITUTES.

" I've been on Newsnight. Shut your face or I'll smash it in, you bell. "

— FRIEDRICH NIETZSCHE

MORE ASTONISHINGLY, JAMIE MACKIE THEN HEADED QPR INTO THE LEAD. TRAUMATIC MEMORIES OF LAST-DAY FAILURES CAME FLOODING BACK FOR CITY FANS.

1983: RELEGATED v LUTON TOWN

1996: TIME-WASTING v LIVERPOOL IN THE MISTAKEN BELIEF THEY'D DONE ENOUGH TO AVOID RELEGATION.

ingenious.

brother

CITY HAMMERED AWAY AT THE QPR GOAL BUT COULDN'T FIND A WAY PAST GOALKEEPER PADDY KENNY.

Air Asia

Air Asia

AS THE GAME MOVED INTO INJURY-TIME, TEARFUL FANS DRIFTED OUT OF THE STADIUM, BELIEVING THAT CITY HAD BLOWN IT AGAIN.

A 92ND MINUTE EDIN DŽEKO EQUALISER GAVE CITY HOPE, BUT AT THAT STAGE THE TITLE WAS STILL GOING TO UNITED. THEY HAD WON 1-0 AT SUNDERLAND, WHERE EVERYONE WAS NOW GLUED TO THEIR PHONES.

FENTON! FENTON!

JESUS CHRIST

FENTON!!

Heh.

THEN, WITH VIRTUALLY THE LAST KICK OF THE SEASON, AGÜERO BURST INTO THE PENALTY AREA AND SMASHED HOME TO SECURE CITY'S FIRST LEAGUE TITLE IN 44 YEARS.

AGUEROOO!!

TRULY, IT WAS A FAIRY TALE ENDING (IF YOUR FAIRY TALE INVOLVES THE PROTAGONIST BEING BANK-ROLLED BY AN EMIRATE PRINCE AND THE LEAD SINGER OF BEADY EYE TURNING UP IN THE FINAL SCENE).

CHAMPIONS 2012 MY PRESENCE GUARANTEES THE SYMPATHY OF NEUTRALS, YOU BELL

'THIS DOES NOT SLIP NOW'
LIVERPOOL BLOW THE 2014 LEAGUE TITLE

Liverpool had just overcome title rivals Manchester City with a breathtaking 3–2 win at Anfield. It was their tenth consecutive win in an unbeaten streak that stretched back to the start of 2014. The players huddle on the pitch, inspirational captain Steven 'Stevie' Gerrard issues an emotional, rousing speech. His immortal words are broadcast into living rooms across the world: 'This does not fucking slip now!'

Another 3–2 win at Norwich the next week left them five points clear with three games to go. Surely now they would end their twenty-four-year wait for a league title. Brendan Rodgers' electrifying side was built on the best middle-management PowerPoint slides available on the internet. Their defence was as durable as Daniel Sturridge's pain threshold and their attack was blessed with the goals of the completely reformed Luis Suárez and the fiercely loyal Raheem Sterling.

Then Chelsea arrived at Anfield. With straightforward-looking matches to follow, a point would have been sufficient for Rodgers' men. But that wasn't the Liverpool way. In the dying seconds of the first half, the ball was played to Gerrard on the edge of the centre circle in his own half. With most of the players in front of him, Gerrard would already have been thinking of launching one of his famously accurate howitzers but, as he took a touch, he slipped. Oh, bitter irony. Chelsea's Demba Ba was on to it in a flash, racing away from a scrambling Gerrard and calmly stroking the ball into the net. The game ended 2–0.

A week later Liverpool were 3–1 up at Crystal Palace with ten minutes to go, but contrived to draw 3–3. Manchester City won their games in hand and leapfrogged them to claim the title. Liverpool were left with only dreams of what might have been and with their captain's prophetic words ringing in their ears.

PERFECTLY RATIONAL BEHAVIOUR FOR A GROWN MAN

LUIS SUÁREZ BITES GIORGIO CHIELLINI

Uruguay manager Oscar Tabárez was right: people *were* always picking on Luis Suárez. Take, for example, the 2010 World Cup. All he'd done there was punch a shot off the line to deny Ghana a clear goal deep in extra-time, then celebrate wildly when the resulting penalty was missed. Clearly he had shown contrition afterwards ('Mine is the real Hand of God. I made the save of the tournament'), but still he was derided as a cheat.

Then there was the biting. People were always on about the biting. You take one little nibble out of another grown adult and everyone loses their mind. OK, so he did it twice. Well, three times if you count the 2014 World Cup (which you shouldn't because *hello, European media conspiracy!*). Who among us can say they haven't sought to achieve an advantage by sinking their teeth into a rival in a workplace environment?

While we're at it, let's clear up the accusations of racism that Suárez has had to endure ever since he repeatedly made pointed references to Patrice Evra's skin colour. This was clearly all a cultural misunderstanding, in that it's part of Evra's culture (Western civilisation in the twenty-first century) to be offended by racism.

Tabárez is right. You should all get over it.

LUIS SUÁREZ ARRIVED AT THE 2014 WORLD CUP WITH SOMETHING OF A REPUTATION. IN ENGLAND, HE HAD RECEIVED A LENGTHY BAN FOR RACIALLY ABUSING PATRICE EVRA, AN UGLY EPISODE, BUT ONE THAT LED TO THE DISCOVERY OF A CURE FOR RACISM.

What you called the traffic warden was reprehensible. I'm sentencing you to score some goals against Norwich, which is apparently sufficient to make everyone forget about it.

SUÁREZ ALSO HAD A WEIRD PENCHANT FOR BITING PEOPLE. HE'D PREVIOUSLY BEEN PUNISHED FOR SINKING HIS TEETH INTO THE FLESH OF PSV'S BAKKAL AND CHELSEA'S BRANISLAV IVANOVIĆ.

Mrs Suárez, I'm afraid Luis has been biting some of the other man-babies. Unless this stops, we'll have to reward him with a multimillion-pound transfer.

If you take it out of his game he'd be half the player.

IT WAS PERHAPS INEVITABLE THAT URUGUAY WOULD BE DRAWN IN THE SAME GROUP AS ENGLAND, THE NATION OF HIS EMPLOYMENT. JUST AS IT WAS INEVITABLE THAT A MISGUIDED HEADER FROM HIS LIVERPOOL TEAM-MATE STEVEN GERRARD WOULD SET HIM UP TO SCORE THE WINNING GOAL.

This does not flick now...

Finally, revenge against all those accursed English journalists who voted me player of the year and wrote endless columns about how lovely I am beneath all the diving and cheating and biting and racisming. Vengeance!

THIS SET UP A DECISIVE FINAL GROUP MATCH AGAINST ITALY. LATE IN THE GAME, WITH THE SCORE DEADLOCKED AT 0-0, SOMETHING SNAPPED IN SUÁREZ'S BRAIN AND HE BIT DOWN INTO GIORGIO CHIELLINI'S SHOULDER.

My teeth! My beautiful teeth!

THE INCIDENT WAS MISSED BY THE REFEREE, BUT FIFA ISSUED HIM WITH AN IMMEDIATE FOUR-MONTH BAN, ENDING HIS WORLD CUP. THANKFULLY, URUGUAY MANAGER ÓSCAR TABÁREZ WAS ON HAND TO REVEAL WHO WAS REALLY TO BLAME.

The British press.

No, not the failure of successive managers to effectively curtail his ill-discipline. Definitely not that.

WHILE SERVING HIS BAN, SUÁREZ SOUGHT PROFESSIONAL HELP AND HAS VOWED TO NEVER BITE ANYONE AGAIN. OPPONENTS CAN REST EASY NOW THAT 'THE HUNGER' HAS BEEN ABATED.

HAHAHAHAHAHAHAHAHAHAHAHAHA!
GERMANY 7 BRAZIL 1

The fourth German goal is the one that really illustrates how completely broken this Brazil team was. Straight from the restart after the third goal, Kroos easily dispossesses Fernandinho, who has the distracted air of a man who suspects he might be on the wrong night bus. Kroos exchanges crisp passes with Khedira and finishes neatly. The Germans barely celebrate, as if it was a training ground exercise against bollards. The television pictures cut to a Brazilian child crying into a soft drink: the perfect metaphor for Brazil's tournament.

As was now traditional, Brazil had been deeply average but had somehow deluded their way through to a semi-final against Germany. Luiz Felipe Scolari's team should have lost to Chile in the second round, then bullied their way past Colombia in the quarter-final. Their physical approach made the Colombians respond in kind. Neymar, their only player of real quality, received a hefty boot to the back, ending his tournament. Their captain, Thiago Silva, would also miss the semi-final through suspension, despite the efforts of the Brazilian FA to overturn his ban. Not to worry, Dante would be drafted into the centre of their defence and he knew all about the German players from his experience with Bayern Munich.

At times, the semi-final was like watching a nature documentary, a slow-motion sequence capturing the beautiful savagery of a crocodile disembowelling a zebra. The other zebras watch on from the sidelines, sobbing into their branded beakers, the rest of the jungle cackling like hyenas, the metaphor overextended.

DANTE'S DIVINE COMEDY

JOIN ME – DANTE! – FOR AN EXPLORATION OF THE NINE CIRCLES OF FUTEBOL HELL.

LIMBO

NEYMAR JR 10

Guys...

Am I...dead?

LUST

Gaze upon my glorious mannschaft. You are powerless to resist its relentless mechanical thrusting.

GLUTTONY

Oh sweet, delicious schadenfreude. More! More!

GREED

Hey man, you don't need all those goals do you? Surely you could spare a few?

Someone else wanting a bail-out from the Germans. Well the bank of Löw ain't open, chum.

ANGER

So long as Brazil keep winning, these fools won't care that we spent the funds for a new hospital on a stadium...

Sir, the microphone.

MAYOR

Get the trebuchet.

HERESY

The Brazilians win a throw-in and fail to drop to their knees and praise me?! Feel my wrath!

VIOLENCE

FRAUD

And what is the purpose of your visit, Mr...?

Fred.

I'm a professional footballer.

TREACHERY

Clearly, Brazilian football has to learn from this defeat and change. So here's our new head coach: the old head coach, Dunga!

CBF

HOUSE OF CADS
FIFA GET RAIDED BY THE FEDS

'I am the president now', roared Sepp Blatter in 2015, 'the president of everyone!' He had just been re-elected the Dark Lord of FIFA, just days after prosecutors had raided a Swiss hotel and arrested a number of his FIFA colleagues. His weird self-denial didn't last long, as even Sepp couldn't face down the list of crimes and misdemeanours revealed by the US Department of Justice.

For decades FIFA had seemed completely indestructible, like the rulers of an undemocratic government too powerful to be overthrown. This cabal of mean old bastards ran football like a private country club, covering their misdeeds with ridiculous double-speak. The extent of their criminality was almost beyond parody. Jack Warner, for example, stands accused of diverting $750,000 intended for the victims of the 2010 Haiti earthquake into his own bank account.

But when FIFA awarded hosting rights for the 2022 World Cup to Qatar – a tiny nation with plenty of money but no football heritage – they managed to create a powerful enemy. The United States had also bid to host that World Cup. Disappointing Greg Dyke is one thing; disappointing Bill Clinton is quite another.

FIFA'S DOWNFALL CAN BE PARTLY TRACED BACK TO ONE MAN: CONCACAF GENERAL SECRETARY, CHUCK BLAZER. HIS TAX RETURN WAS AT ODDS WITH HIS EXTRAVAGANT LIFESTYLE, WHICH EVEN INCLUDED RENTING AN APARTMENT IN 'TRUMP TOWER' FOR HIS CATS.

HE WAS EN ROUTE TO A RESTAURANT ON HIS MOBILITY SCOOTER WHEN ARRESTED BY THE FBI AND IRS.

Pretty fancy place for a man of your limited means, Chuck.

Wagyu beef.

Pure.

HE WAS CONVINCED TO WORK WITH INVESTIGATORS TO GATHER EVIDENCE OF FIFA WRONGDOING, WHICH HE DID FOR TWO YEARS.

Hey Chuck, your macaw is making a whirring sound. It's putting me off my corruptioning, I have to say.

He's got bronchitis.

They're on to me, I know it! I can't do this no more, man!

Hey! Post-retirement Letterman, you're done when we say.

THE EVIDENCE HE COLLECTED LED TO THE DRAMATIC ARRESTS OF 14 FIFA EXECUTIVES AT A SWISS HOTEL IN MAY 2015, WITH FURTHER INDICTMENTS IN THE MONTHS THAT FOLLOWED.

To be fair, he arrived like that too. It's pretty shameful being a FIFA exec.

PRESIDENT SEPP BLATTER CLUNG ON TO POWER FOR A SHORT TIME, BUT WAS EVENTUALLY BANNED BY FIFA. AT THE END, HE CUT A SAD FIGURE, A STICKY PLASTER COVERING THE VOICE OF HIS CONSCIENCE, WHICH HAD TAKEN ON PHYSICAL FORM.

They're on to you. You're done, Blatty, done!

FIFA TODAY IS UNDER NEW LEADERSHIP AND, AS YOU READ THIS, IT IS NO DOUBT HAILED AS A BASTION OF TRUTH, TRANSPARENCY AND INTEGRITY. JUST AS CHUCK BLAZER IS NOW PROBABLY PLAYING IN CENTRAL MIDFIELD FOR REAL MADRID.

HOWEVER, THE FATE OF THE CATS IN THE TRUMP TOWER APARTMENT REMAINS A MYSTERY.

A baseless boast followed by some lowest common denominator insults about immigrants or women. Pause for applause. Yeah.

FOXES IN THE CHICKEN COOP
LEICESTER CITY WIN THE PREMIER LEAGUE

2016. A year of chaos, confusion and death. Once David Bowie passed away, the very foundations of civilised society began to crumble. Yet among the depressing news of mass murder, celebrity mortality and James Corden's Carpool Karaoke, there was one bright spark of positivity: Leicester City won the Premier League. *Leicester.* The Foxes' pre-season preparations gave no indication of what was to follow. Their best player, Esteban Cambiasso, had cleared off; three young players were sacked after appearing in a 'racist sex tape' during a tour of Thailand; striker Jamie Vardy was sanctioned after being caught on film racially abusing a Japanese man in a casino; and manager Nigel Pearson was fired. His replacement, Claudio Ranieri, arrived with his reputation in tatters after a dire spell as the manager of Greece.

But then something strange happened: Leicester started winning. In fact, they only lost one match between the start of the season and Christmas. Their high-energy game was anchored by the defensive stoicism of Wes Morgan and Robert Huth, with new signing N'Golo Kanté emerging as one of the most impressive midfielders in Europe. On the wing Riyad Mahrez performed with such consistency that he would become PFA Player of the Year. And then there was Jamie Vardy.

Vardy broke the Premier League record for scoring in consecutive matches (eleven), a stunning achievement for someone who had been playing non-league football only a few years earlier.

As the season progressed and they stood firm at the top of the table as traditional challengers faltered. José Mourinho's Chelsea publically cannibalised themselves, Manchester City played as if their manager was leaving at the end of the season, Arsenal were Arsenal and Louis van Gaal's Manchester United were insipid. Tottenham were the only club to push Leicester to the title, tellingly.

Leicester secured the title with two games to spare, their remarkable story was an inspiration to clubs across the land; an example of what could be achieved with a strong work ethic, a motivated set of players and a cosy sponsorship deal with a Thai billionaire. Truly, it was a fairy tale.

STADIUMS IN THE SKY
THE FUTURE OF FOOTBALL

The winger darts down the touchline in his rocket boots, the ball at his feet, the roar of the hologram crowd blows back his post-punk hairstyle. Through his visor, he is informed that the space car he ordered is being beamed to his gravity-free garage or something. Although it cost 12 million TrumpTokens, this pleases him; an emotion that is immediately expressed via the digital emoji display that has replaced his face.

His visor also informs him that a team-mate has found space in the penalty area. The striker is a foreign import from Quadrant F and is a gas-based life form and is therefore a nightmare for defenders. The winger swings a perfect cross into the penalty zone, the vaporous centre-forward must score. But then, disaster: being a yellow cloud, it lacks the physical presence to control the ball, which rolls out for a kick-in. Another disappointing afternoon for Chamakh Five.

The year is 2019 and you are at a Premier League game. *On the moon.* Well, your hologram is. You're at home, having your organs juiced for space car lubricant. You need the TrumpTokens.

The Future of Football

EVERYONE AGREES THAT TELEVISION DOESN'T HAVE ENOUGH POWER OVER FOOTBALL. VIDEO TECHNOLOGY IS INTRODUCED AND FOR AN 'ASPIRATIONAL' SUBSCRIPTION FEE, CONSUMERS CAN VOTE ON KEY IN-GAME DECISIONS.

Oops, wrong app. I think I've just crushed the fourth official with a giant digital lemon.

THE BIG EUROPEAN CLUBS FINALLY FREE THEMSELVES FROM THE TYRANNY OF MERITOCRACY. THEY FORM THEIR OWN EXHIBITION TOURNAMENT THAT BOASTS ALL THE DRAMATIC TENSION OF WATCHING THE HARLEM FUCKING GLOBETROTTERS.

'MARKET FORCES' PUT TICKET COSTS BEYOND THE MEANS OF MOST FANS. LOOK, IF YOU WANT TO WATCH PLAYERS OF THE CALIBRE OF JORDAN HENDERSON, YOU HAVE TO EXPECT A PRICE HIKE. UNSOLD SEATS ARE REPLACED WITH PREMIUM ADVERTISING SPACE.

LOAN CASINO

BORROW THEN BET THEN BORROW!

THE INEVITABLE CONSEQUENCES OF CLIMATE CHANGE CREATE A BOLD NEW LOOK FOR FOOTBALL KITS. PERSONALISED OXYGEN TANKS AND FLIPPERS BECOME DE RIGUEUR.

If global warming is real then how come this sea is cold? It's a greenie socialist conspiracy!

ADVANCES IN VIRTUAL REALITY TECHNOLOGY ALLOW PEOPLE TO EXPERIENCE FIRST-HAND THE THRILLS AND SPILLS OF PROFESSIONAL FOOTBALL.

Two pickled eggs and a battered saveloy please, love.

RACISM, SEXISM AND HOMOPHOBIA ARE ERADICATED FROM FOOTBALL AS THOUSANDS OF YEARS OF SCROLLING THROUGH THEIR PHONES LEADS TO HUMANS EVOLVING INTO IDENTICAL GIANT SEXLESS THUMBS.

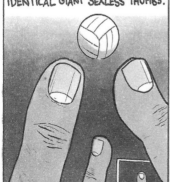

IN FIVE BILLION YEARS, THE DYING SUN EXPANDS, BOILING THE EARTH'S OCEANS AND ENGULFING THE PLANET IN A WALL OF FIRE. ARSENAL FINISH THIRD AGAIN.

In a way it's like winning a trophy.

BUT NO MATTER WHAT HAPPENS IN THE MEANTIME, OUR INNATE DESIRE TO KICK A ROUND OBJECT WILL ABIDE AND THE LOVE OF FOOTBALL WILL LIVE ON.

BIBLIOGRAPHY

Books

Phil Ball, *Morbo*

Patrick Barclay, *The Life and Times of Herbert Chapman*

Alex Bellos, *Futebol*

Paul Brown, *The Victorian Football Miscellany*

David Conn, *The Beautiful Game?*

David Conn, *Richer than God*

Jack Charlton, *The Autobiography*

Kevin Connolly and Rab McWilliam, *Fields of Glory, Paths of Gold*

Jeff Dawson, *Back Home*

John Foot, *Calcio*

Cris Freddi, *The Complete Book of the World Cup*

Brian Glanville, *For Club and Country*

Brian Glanville, *The Story of the World Cup*

David Goldblatt, *The Ball Is Round*

Duncan Hamilton, *Provided You Don't Kiss Me*

Ian Hawkey, *Feet of the Chameleon*

Uli Hesse, *Tor!*

Christ Hunt, *World Cup Stories*

Hyder Jawad, *Four Weeks in Montevideo*

Roy Keane, *Keane*

Simon Kuper, *Football Against The Enemy*

Simon Kuper and Stefan Szymanski, *Soccernomics*

Amy Lawrence, *Invincible*

Diego Maradona, *El Diego*

Andrea Pirlo, *I Think Therefore I Play*

Ian Plenderleith, *Rock 'n' Roll Soccer*

Bobby Robson, *Farewell But Not Goodbye*

Peter Seddon, *The World Cup's Strangest Moments*

John Spurling, *Death or Glory*

David Wangerin, *Soccer in a Football World*

Jonathan Wilson, *The Anatomy of England*

Jonathan Wilson, *Inverting the Pyramid*
Jonathan Wilson with Scott Murray, *The Anatomy of Liverpool*
David Winner, *Brilliant Orange*
David Winner, *Those Feet*

Magazines
When Saturday Comes, Issue 210, Paul Pomonis, 'Accidental Heroes'
When Saturday Comes, Issue 338, John Spurling, 'Exit Strategy'
The Blizzard

Websites
www.bbc.com
www.beyondthelastman.com
www.bleacherreport.com
www.chrishunt.biz
www.dailymail.co.uk
www.espnfc.com
www.fourfourtwo.com
www.theguardian.com
www.inbedwithmaradona.com
www.independent.co.uk
www.liverpoolecho.co.uk
www.nytimes.com
www.pitchinvasion.net
www.reuters.com
www.sbnation.com
www.si.com
www.standard.co.uk
www.spiegel.de
www.telegraph.co.uk
www.thepfa.com
www.twohundredpercent.net
www.uefa.com
www.worldsoccer.com
www.youtube.com

ACKNOWLEDGEMENTS

As with most books, this one wasn't written in isolation and it wouldn't have been possible without the work and guidance of a load of fantastic people, who I'd like to tip my hat to here.

Firstly, I'd like to thank my representative, Iain Macintosh, who approached me in early 2015 with the offer of touting my name around a few publishers. This must have been a leap of faith on Iain's part, as he had no idea about me beyond my cartoons in the *Guardian*. It was only later that he discovered I am a compulsive worrier, but I already had his email address by then.

I'd also like to thank Ian Prior at the *Guardian*, who took a punt on commissioning me to provide a weekly cartoon and stuck with me even after the very first one I published contained a glaring typo. Ian and the rest of the *Guardian* Sports team (particularly James Dart, who spares me from any further typo-related mishaps on a weekly basis) have been endlessly supportive over the last couple of years and I can't express my gratitude enough. Equally, Mike Hytner at *Guardian* Australia has been an absolute bloody ripper and has often helped me work through moments of self-doubt. It is a testament to his character that he was able to forgive me getting his surname wrong for the first year of our working relationship.

I also owe a debt of gratitude to Ben Brusey and Huw Armstrong at Penguin Random House. Their editorial direction and much-welcomed encouragement have enabled this book to be as good as it could possibly be. They have been an absolute delight to work with, so much so that I am even able to forgive Ben for being a Reading fan.

I'm legally obliged to acknowledge the musicians whose lyrics are quoted in this book: The Shamen ('Love, Sex, Intelligence'), Robbie Williams ('Let Me Entertain You') and MIMS ('This Is Why I'm Hot'). Please note, MIMS should not be confused with the former Everton and Blackburn Rovers goalkeeper, Bobby Mimms, who, to the best of my knowledge, is not, and has never been, hot.

Thanks also to my family and friends who have helped me through this long process, either through providing advice and information, or by simply being there to listen to me rant on about not being able to think of a good joke about Bayern Munich's team of the mid-1970s. Special mentions to: Pete

Barber, Simon Hodgon, Kieran Holden, John Mitchell, Jonathan O'Shea, Ian Plenderleith, Justin Smith, David Stubbs, Paul Whitehead and Alastair Wilson. Also thanks to the online community at *When Saturday Comes*, who have backed my cartoon work since the outset and can rightly complain about the bloody fair-weather fans who have only discovered my stuff more recently.

OK, this is starting to sound like the longest pre-Thanksgiving-dinner prayer in history (and I only know about that from my consumption of American television). I'll wrap up by thanking my parents, for their endless support and love and, most importantly, by thanking my partner, Sarah. There aren't many people who would have stuck by someone who spent over a year of their relationship hunched over a drawing board, and she has to be one of the most patient people on the planet. This book simply wouldn't have happened without her. Thank you, Sarah.

Right, you can eat now, tuck in.